War of 1812
UPDATED EDITION

MIRIAM GREENBLATT

JOHN S. BOWMAN
GENERAL EDITOR

Facts On File, Inc.

Note on Photos
Many of the illustrations and photographs used in this book are old,
historical images. The quality of the prints is not always up to modern
standards, as in some cases the originals are from glass negatives or are damaged.
The content of the illustrations, however, made their inclusion important
despite problems in reproduction.

Facts On File, Inc.
132 West 31st Street
New York NY 10001

Library of Congress Cataloging-in-Publication Data
Greenblatt, Miriam.
War of 1812 / by Miriam Greenblatt.— Updated ed.
p. cm. — (America at war)
Summary: A revised account of the events surrounding the War of 1812
between the newly established United States and Great Britain.
Includes bibliographical references and index.
ISBN 0-8160-4933-5
1. United States—History—War of 1812—Juvenile literature. [1. United States—
History—War of 1812.] I. Title. II. Series.
E354 .G74 2003
973.5'2—dc21   2002009555

Facts On File books are available at special discounts when purchased in bulk
quantities for businesses, associations, institutions, or sales promotions. Please call our
Special Sales Department in New York at (212) 967-8800 or (800) 322-8755.

You can find Facts On File on the World Wide Web at http://www.factsonfile.com

Text design by Erika K. Arroyo
Logo design by Smart Graphics
Maps by Jeremy Eagle

Printed in the United States of America

MP FOF 10 9 8 7 6 5 4 3 2 1

This book is printed on acid-free paper.

Contents

Preface

It has often been said that every generation writes its own history. In modern times, with the invention of satellites, computers, and similar devices, it sometimes seems as if history is rewritten every decade. That is certainly true about the War of 1812. Since the first edition of this book was published in 1994, historians have made several significant changes in their views and accounts of the conflict.

Among the most significant of these changes is an emphasis on the part played by African-American soldiers and sailors. In the past, the contributions of this group to America's early wars were rarely touched upon. Few students of history were even aware, for example, that one out of seven Americans who fought with George Washington in the Revolutionary War was a free black. Although the first edition of *War of 1812* described the role of African-Americans in the Battle of Bladensburg, the current edition also contains information about black sailors at the Battle of Lake Erie and black soldiers at the Battle of New Orleans. It is interesting to note that black sailors were active on the opposing side of the war as well. There were black sailors in Britain's Royal Navy and black marines among the British troops that marched on Washington, D.C., in 1814.

Another change in the treatment of the War of 1812 has to do with Native Americans. In the past, historians seldom described how the war destroyed the Indians' hopes for maintaining their way of life in the eastern part of North America. Today, historians discuss this development at considerable length. The current edition of *War of 1812,* for example, includes both a map and a detailed account of Indian removal from the lands east of the Mississippi to those west of the river.

The issue is not static, however. Robert Remini—probably America's leading scholar on Andrew Jackson and his time—recently presented a new analysis of Indian removal. In *Andrew Jackson and His Indian Wars,*

Remini takes a different approach. He acknowledges the fact that white settlers were constantly encroaching on Indian land, but he argues that Indian removal was the only feasible solution. Genocide was not acceptable. Whites did not favor integration, and, for that matter, most Native Americans did not want to integrate into white society. The United States either broke the treaties it signed with various tribes or failed to enforce the treaties and protect the Native Americans against squatters. Accordingly, if the Indians were to survive at all, they would have to move west of the Mississippi River. In other words, Remini contends that Jackson's policy of Indian removal "saved the Five Civilized Nations from probable extinction." Remini's thesis is undoubtedly controversial, but it is bound to be widely discussed and evaluated during the coming years.

Another consequence of the War of 1812 that seems ripe for discussion is the demise of the Federalist Party and the effect this had on national politics. The party had come into being when Americans were debating whether or not to ratify the Constitution. In general, Federalists favored a strong central government and were among the nation's best educated and wealthiest men. They also favored Britain over France.

The downfall of the Federalist Party began in earnest in 1812. In that year, the Federalists concluded that they had no chance of electing a president in wartime. Accordingly, instead of running a candidate of their own, they threw their support to Dewitt Clinton of New York, who had been nominated by minority Republicans to run against James Madison. Although the Federalists campaigned energetically, the Electoral College favored Madison over Clinton by a vote of 128 to 89. Perhaps the most significant aspect of the vote was the fact that the Electoral College split on a regional basis. Delegates from New England supported Clinton; delegates from the South and West voted solidly for Madison.

Federalist opposition to a conflict with Great Britain had grown as a result of Jefferson's embargo, which ruined New England's trade and its economic prosperity before becoming a dead letter by 1812. As the war continued without either side gaining the upper hand, Federalist opposition increased still further. There were mutterings about secession and even some proposals for a separate peace between New England and Great Britain. Although the Hartford Convention of 1814–15 rejected both ideas, convention members endorsed seven changes in the U.S. Constitution that would have strengthened the political power of New England Federalists and undermined that of the Republican South and West.

PREFACE

As matters turned out, Andrew Jackson's victory at New Orleans, combined with the signing of a peace treaty at Ghent, made the Federalists appear, as one historian wrote, "ridiculous if not treasonous." As American nationalism increased after the war, the power of the Federalists went into a rapid decline. By the 1820s, the Federalist Party was no more. Such a result might well inspire discussions of the "unintended consequences" of other wars in the history of the United States.

Yet despite the Federalists' demise, the issue of regionalism they had raised grew stronger as the years went by. It became clearer that different regions of the United States had different economic interests. One example was the protective tariff of 1816, which levied taxes on such imports as cottons, woolens, leather, iron, and sugar. Southern congressmen objected because the tariff raised the prices that southern families had to pay for imported goods. Most northern congressmen favored the tariff because it encouraged the production of iron and cloth in their areas. Such regional disputes would eventually play an important part in the outbreak of the Civil War.

In addition to modifying their accounts of the War of 1812, historians over the past several years have begun to point out resonances between the war and current events. One such has to do with Jefferson's embargo. It was originally designed as a form of "peaceable coercion," a way to avoid direct conflict between American merchant ships and British and French warships. Although the embargo was temporarily successful, it had unintended consequences that harmed the United States, namely, a loss of trade and an economic depression. These soon led to the embargo's collapse.

A contemporary example of just such an embargo is the one that the United States began to enforce against Cuba in 1961. Cuba, of course, never represented more than a fraction of U.S. export-import trade, and there is no denying that over the decades the embargo has hurt Cuba's economy far more than that of the United States. But in later years, with the end of the cold war and the Soviet Union's withdrawal as Cuba's chief economic supporter, numerous foreign countries—including Canada— began to ignore the embargo and commence trading operations with Cuba. And so, just as the New England manufacturers chafed at the restrictions of Jefferson's embargo, so increasing numbers of U.S. manufacturers and exporters of products desired by Cubans began to chafe at this policy of "peaceable coercion." These people may or may not be concerned whether the embargo has weakened or strengthened Fidel

Castro's hold on his fellow Cubans; what they do fear is that they are losing out in the race to play a role in the Cuban economy of the future.

Following the Persian Gulf War of 1991, the United States again adopted "peaceable coercion" as a strategic technique. It levied an embargo on trade with Iraq and declared that sanctions would not be lifted until Iraq showed that it was not developing nuclear, chemical, or biological weapons. Iraq, however, refused to allow international inspectors to see all that they wanted, and many experts believe that Iraq has secretly continued to stockpile nuclear bombs and chemical and biological weapons. At the same time, observers point out that an unintended consequence of that embargo has been a sharp increase in the death rate among Iraqi children and old people resulting from a shortage of food, fresh water, and medical supplies. It is estimated that nearly 1 million Iraqis have perished. Yet Saddam Hussein remains in power. Although the trade embargo on Iraq has not damaged America's economy, it has led many historians to question whether "peaceable coercion" is in fact a desirable technique for the United States to employ.

Several additional resonances between the War of 1812 and the present have resulted from the September 11, 2001, terrorist attacks against Washington, D.C., and New York City. The most obvious, of course, has to do with the attack on the Pentagon and the White House. Once again, an enemy struck at major symbols of U.S. national government. Although there was far greater loss of life, the physical damage in Washington was much less extensive than what occurred during the War of 1812. Then, almost every government building in the capital was burned; the president and his cabinet, together with Congress, evacuated the city; and most of Washington's inhabitants sought safety elsewhere. This time, the attack on the White House was thwarted, while the Pentagon was only partially damaged. Although some government workers had to change their offices, business went on as usual. Nevertheless, the symbolism was the same.

A second obvious resonance is between President George W. Bush's declaration of a "war on terrorism" and what historian Kevin Baker has called "our first fight against international terrorists." Baker points out that before and after the War of 1812, the United States sent warships over thousands of miles to attack the Barbary States of Tripoli, Tunis, Algiers, and Morocco, whose various rulers had seized U.S. ships and imprisoned or enslaved American sailors. It took three decades before the United States was able to, as Baker said, "put an end to the random slaughter and harassment of American citizens." But the United States succeeded and, in the process, strengthened its navy and established the U.S. Marine Corps. Both the Barbary States and the Marine Corps are discussed in the new edition of this book.

Still another resonance between the War of 1812 and the present has to do with the reasons for the September 11, 2001, attacks. Observers have advanced numerous possible explanations of why al-Qaeda targeted the United States. One is Muslim resentment over the present low status of most Muslim states as compared with their high status in the past, when the Persian, Arab, and Ottoman Empires were among the most powerful in the world, as well as leaders in science and art. A second proposed reason is the support the United States has given the governments of many Muslim nations that are in fact corrupt, repressive, and indifferent to the needs of their people. A third reason that has been advanced is the presence of U.S. troops in Saudi Arabia, home of the Muslim holy cities of Mecca and Medina. A fourth reason proffered is American support for the Israelis in their struggle with the Palestinians. A fifth proposed reason is that Osama bin Laden wants to establish a fundamentalist Islamic state encompassing the entire Middle East, with himself as its ruler.

A broader explanation for the events of September 11 may be, as historian Karen Armstrong has written, that the Muslim world is passing through the so-called Great Western Transformation in which a traditional agrarian society becomes modern—that is, it becomes a society based on technology and capital reinvestment that is also democratic and religiously tolerant. One of the side effects of modernization is that religious fundamentalists often feel their values are under attack. So they lash out, according to Armstrong, "at first against one's own countrymen or co-religionists," and then against some foreign enemy whom they blame for their country's ills.

What does all this have to do with the War of 1812? According to an article by military historian Caleb Carr, the reason for the terrorist attacks of September 11 replicates the reason for the outbreak of the War of 1812. Carr does not agree with those historians who list specific political grievances or economic rivalries; quite the contrary. He argues that what set off the 1812 conflict was "a deep anxiety over the spread of American democratic republicanism." In other words, Great Britain—an imperial nation with a stratified social and political structure—was afraid that its former colony would set an example for uprisings in its overseas possessions and even at home. And in fact, Carr argues, the United States *did* lead the way to ending British colonialism and imperialism. Today, as in 1812, Carr asserts, it is opposition to the spread of American values that animates enemies of the United States.

But beyond such new interpretations, emphases, and resonances, this edition of *War of 1812* offers several other features that enhance its value and appeal to both teachers and readers. There are more illustrations and maps. The recommended reading list is considerably larger, offering not only more current works of nonfiction but also a selection of fiction related to the war. (Although the Horatio Hornblower novels of C. S. Forester do not qualify for this list, since they do not actually involve the War of 1812, they provide some of the most vivid and realistic descriptions of naval battles during this period.) Another new element is the glossary, which provides definitions of the many specialized words and terms used throughout the text. Finally, there are the box features that open windows onto a variety of topics that may lie outside the main narrative but nonetheless add new dimensions to the history of this war.

Not all readers will follow all the issues raised by this book. What they show, however, is that the past informs the present and that the War of 1812 is surprisingly relevant almost 200 years later. The converse is that readers of this volume should bring more perspectives than ever to the War of 1812.

1

"THE DARKEST DAY"

When the residents of Washington, D.C., picked up their copies of the *National Intelligencer* on August 16, 1814, they saw a startling news item:

> By express from Norfolk, 11 o'clock—A list of vessels has appeared . . . 10 miles to the southward of Cape Henry [Virginia]: 5 seventy-fours, 6 frigates, 1 sloop-of-war, 10 transports, 1 tender. . . .
>
> 1 o'clock, p.m.—Another express: the fleet have all come in from the Capes and gone up Chesapeake Bay.

By the following morning, the number of ships in the British fleet had more than doubled to 51. And judging from the type of ships, it was clear that the British were preparing for an invasion. A seventy-four was a ship of the line, or battleship, that carried from 64 to 120 cannons mounted on three gundecks. Although slow and clumsy, its firepower was so great that it could be stopped only by another battleship. A frigate, which carried between 32 and 44 cannons mounted on a single deck, was used mostly for hunting enemy merchant ships. A sloop-of-war, armed with 16 to 24 cannons, was fast-moving and ideal for blockading harbor entrances. A transport carried troops, while a tender carried supplies.

Yet despite the British fleet's appearance, most Washingtonians remained unconcerned. They found it hard to believe that they were really in danger. For one thing, the war between the United States and Great Britain had been going on for more than two years, and all the battles to date had taken place far away—either on the high seas, on the

Great Lakes, or west of the Allegheny Mountains. Then, too, even the British must know that August was an awful month for fighting near the capital! Temperatures along the Potomac and Patuxent Rivers usually hovered around 100 degrees, while the equally high humidity made staying in the shade the only sensible thing to do. In addition, on July 2, President James Madison had moved to protect the capital by setting up a new military district.

The 10th Military District covered northern Virginia, Maryland, and the District of Columbia and was commanded by Brig. Gen. William Henry Winder. Some people considered him a poor choice. A Baltimore lawyer in peacetime, he had no military background. Since this war began in 1812, he had fought in just one battle, during which he had been made a prisoner and only recently exchanged. On the other hand, he was both amiable and available—and his uncle was Governor Levin Winder of Maryland. That was an important consideration.

At the time, the bulk of the U.S. Army was made up not of regular soldiers but of militiamen from the individual states—in other words, farmers, merchants, mechanics, and clerks who had been called up by their state governors. Unfortunately, most governors were reluctant to have their militia serve outside their own state borders. This meant that the defense of Washington fell mostly on the Maryland militia. And although Governor Winder had not been in favor of the war, it was unthinkable that he would let his nephew down by withholding military support.

Nevertheless, General Winder faced an almost impossible task. The capital lacked defensive fortifications. Secretary of War John Armstrong ignored his pleas for rifles, flints, tents, and wagons. Armstrong was convinced the British would never attack Washington. "[It] won't win the war," he said. "There is no need for worry. . . . Baltimore is the place." Winder himself seemed incapable of organizing a military staff or devising a plan of action. He spent most of his time dashing around the countryside and fussing over trivia, such as who should have first call on a clerk's services.

Then, on August 19, some 4,500 battle-hardened British troops—led by Irish-born major general Robert Ross—disembarked from their ships at the village of Benedict near the mouth of the Patuxent River. There was no resistance. In fact, not a single American made an appearance, not even to reconnoiter. The next day, the British troops began moving toward Washington, some 40 miles away.

The march was very uncomfortable. Heat waves shimmered in the air. Dust rose from the ground as the soldiers moved along and flew into their faces and between their teeth. The men were soft from being cooped

The Nation's Capital

ONE OF THE FIRST QUESTIONS THAT AROSE AFTER THE establishment of the United States was where to locate the capital. The Continental Congress had met in Philadelphia, New York, and half a dozen other cities. The U.S. Congress, however, felt that a new nation should have a new capital.

The next question was where to build it. Northern states did not want it in the southern slaveholding states. Southern states did not want it in the North. Congressmen wanted it in some quiet place "far removed from crowds of complaining citizens." And it had to be on a navigable waterway in order to encourage trade.

An agreement was finally reached to place the new capital on the Potomac River, about midway between the northern and southern boundaries of the United States. In 1790 George Washington chose a 10-mile-square site on the river's east bank, to be called the District of Columbia (named for Christopher Columbus). The following year, he commissioned French engineer Pierre Charles L'Enfant to draw up a plan for the city. (It was named Washington only after his death, in December 1799.)

L'Enfant's design called for square blocks, some of them cut by diagonal streets so as to form public squares. It also called for wide thoroughfares. Streets were to be 100 feet wide and avenues 160 feet wide. The main boulevard, now Pennsylvania Avenue, was to be 400 feet wide. It was to run for almost two miles, from the Capitol building, which was placed on a hill near the center of town, to the President's House, now known as the White House.

By 1800, enough public buildings had been completed for John Adams to transfer the federal government from Philadelphia to Washington. Most of L'Enfant's plan, however, was not put into effect until after the Civil War. So the city that the British burned in 1812 was shabby and unimpressive. Small frame houses, stables, and badly designed government buildings were scattered along Pennsylvania Avenue. The avenue itself was unpaved. Cows and pigs wandered about, while only weeds grew in the places that had been set aside for parks. The British torched the capital, but it damaged national pride more than impressive buildings.

up aboard ship. They were also heavily laden. As British subaltern (lieutenant) George Robert Gleig reported later:

> The load which they carried likewise was far from trifling. [Probably thirty pounds a least.] Independent of their arms and sixty rounds of ball cartridge, each man bore upon his back a knapsack containing shirts, shoes, stockings, etc., a blanket, a haversack with provisions for three days, and a canteen or wooden keg filled with water.

To make matters worse, the British employed the so-called Moore Quickstep—three steps at a run, then three steps at a walk. Dozens of redcoats, unable to keep up the pace, fell behind, while about 60 dropped dead from exhaustion, sunstroke, or heart failure. Nevertheless, the troops pressed on.

That night they camped in some cultivated cornfields, where for the first time they experienced an American thunderstorm. It was very different from the mild English storms to which they were accustomed. Rain poured down for two hours, while lightning streaked across the sky and the thunder "echoed back . . . from the thick woods around." Subaltern Gleig observed that the effect of the lightning as it illuminated the soldiers and the weapons piled by their side "was extremely fine." However, "the effect of the rain was not so agreeable for, being perfectly destitute of shelter, we were speedily wet to the skin."

British troops invading Washington, D.C., met with little resistance from unprepared Americans. *(Library of Congress)*

"THE DARKEST DAY"

Joshua Barney, commander of the Chesapeake fleet, destroyed his ships to distract the British. *(Library of Congress)*

At daybreak of August 21, the British reformed their line of march and continued northward. That afternoon they had their first skirmish with American troops, in a thick forest near the town of Nottingham. The skirmish did not last long. After a few minutes of thunderous firing, the American riflemen took to their heels. Casualties were almost non-existent: one American was killed, while the British soldiers did not even suffer a scratch. That evening the British camped in Nottingham, which they found completely deserted. The next morning they resumed their march, toward Upper Marlboro, a town some 20 miles southeast of Washington, D.C.

As the British army advanced, the British naval forces—commanded by Rear Adm. George Cockburn (pronounced "Coburn")—also went into action. The ships of the fleet were too big to sail into the headwaters of the Patuxent. So Cockburn—a ruthless officer who began his naval career as a cabin boy at the age of nine—transferred three units of marines, together with artillery, into some 40 small barges. Slowly they rowed upstream. Their goal was to find and attack the American Chesapeake fleet commanded by Commodore Joshua Barney. This consisted of one sloop-of-war, the *Scorpion,* and 16 old scows (flat-bottomed boats) on which guns had been mounted.

WAR OF 1812

On August 22, just below the village of Pig Point, where the Patuxent is little more than a stream, the British came upon Barney's fleet. It was strung out in a line, the *Scorpion* at the head flying a pennant, then the 16 gunboats, and behind them a huddle of 13 trading schooners laden with tobacco. But before the British could make a move, smoke began pouring from the *Scorpion,* and a few seconds later the American flagship blew up. Then the gunboats—including an ammunition boat—began exploding too. The British were able to capture only one of the ships—and not a single gun. Commodore Barney had removed all the cannons the previous night. Then he had taken 400 of his sailors and marines and set out to join General Winder, leaving behind a few flotillamen to scuttle his ships when the British appeared.

By this time, the Americans—finally awake to the British threat to Washington—had taken several steps to protect the capital. On August 21, Mayor James H. Blake posted the following notice:

All able-bodied Citizens remaining here and all free-men of color, are required to convene tomorrow morning at 6 o'clock precisely, at the Capitol—and from thence to proceed to a site near Bladensburg [along the Potomac's east branch, about 5 miles from Washington], to throw up a breastwork or redoubt, deemed important by the Commanding General, for the defense of our city. Those who cannot attend in person, will please send substitutes.

Shovels, spades and pick-axes will be furnished on the spot.

Each man must take his provisions for the day with him.

The following day, the *National Intelligencer* reported that "An immense crowd (supposed to amount to 4 or 5 hundred) of every description of persons, attended to offer their services."

By this time, too, General Winder had set up a military command at the Wood Yard near Bladensburg. As of August 22, his force numbered about 3,000 infantry, 425 cavalry, and 20 guns. Another 4,000 reinforcements were expected to arrive the following day. Unfortunately, neither the troops nor their commander really knew what they were doing. As U.S. Army Brigade Maj. John S. Williams pointed out:

The militia troops under Gen. Winder were mostly without any training or discipline whatever—men drafted from peaceable walks of life, in a peaceable section of the country, habituated to comforts and conveniences, to regular hours and good living, instead of being inured to danger or privation. They were unaccustomed to subordination, and disposed to treat their commanding officers as associates and equals.

Whatever their capacities might have been, there was no time to draw them out; and whatever the qualifications of their officers they were, with but exceptions, wholly unknown to the commanding general who was therefore unable to designate, for the performance of any particular duty, those who might have been capable of performing it. He could not be sure that any order would be promptly executed or any duty properly performed.

Not that Winder had any clear notion of what orders to issue. For example, on August 22, he rode out from the Wood Yard to a nearby ridge from which he could observe the British invaders marching along. But instead of sending out soldiers to harass and delay the enemy, Winder decided to fall back to Long Old Fields, five miles nearer Washington. There, he spent the rest of the day and most of the evening doing paperwork.

The camp itself was thoroughly disorganized. As one historian described it:

> Nobody seemed to know what was going on. Militiamen wandered about, filling the air with coarse shouting and quarrelsome phrases, and there were dozens of fist fights. The pickets were sloppy and trigger-happy; soldiers coming into the camp stopped at a safe distance to shout the countersign lest they catch a bullet from the impetuous guards.

Conditions in Washington, D.C., were equally chaotic. Children ran through the streets while their mothers searched for carts, wagons, anything on wheels to get out of the city. Government officials packed records from the State Department in coarse linen sacks for shipment to safety in Virginia. Among the documents were a copy of the Declaration of Independence, the Articles of Confederation, the U.S. Constitution, and George Washington's commission as commander in chief of the Continental army. A few fortunate individuals managed to store their valuables in the house of French minister Louis Serurier, who held diplomatic immunity. Most people, though, simply abandoned their furniture and other possessions and fled.

At 8:00 A.M. on August 23, President James Madison, accompanied by other dignitaries, rode out to review the American troops. They were an unimpressive sight. Only about half wore uniforms, and many carried tomahawks because they lacked muskets. Still, as editor Joseph Gales of the *National Intelligencer* observed, they were "all in fine spirits." Gales's account marked the first time that an American war correspondent reported events from the front.

After the review, Madison held a council of war. The president felt that the British, having destroyed Barney's flotilla, would return to their ships. General Winder believed the British would attack Fort Washington, on the Potomac near Alexandria, before moving against the capital. Secretary of War Armstrong was convinced that "If an attack is meditated by them upon any place, it is Annapolis." At noon, a scout galloped up with a report that the British army was still camped at the town of Upper Marlboro. That made Madison's theory more likely. It also seemed probable that the British would do nothing that afternoon. So Madison returned to the capital after the council decided that the Americans would themselves attack the British at Upper Marlboro the following day. Winder meanwhile mounted his horse and headed for Bladensburg, where some of his troops had dug in.

At two o'clock that afternoon, as Winder neared Bladensburg, he heard gunfire coming from the direction of Upper Marlboro. Just a skirmish between American scouts and enemy pickets, he decided. But he was wrong. It was the entire British army—and it was marching straight toward Washington!

Panic-stricken, Winder turned around and galloped back to Long Old Fields. What should he do now? Should he fight where he was? But suppose the British mounted an assault in the dark. True, they had never done that, and they were unfamiliar with the terrain. But in a night fight, the Americans would be unable to use their artillery. Perhaps he should combine the troops at Long Old Fields with those at Bladensburg and fight the British there? But that would leave open the road to Washington across the east branch of the Potomac. And suppose no one obeyed his orders to burn the two bridges across the river if they saw the British coming? Then the enemy would simply walk into the nation's capital!

So once again, General Winder made a foolish decision. He ordered the American forces at Long Old Fields to pull back to Washington.

The retreat turned into a disorderly flight. It was, as artilleryman John Law put it, "a run of eight miles." When the exhausted men reached their

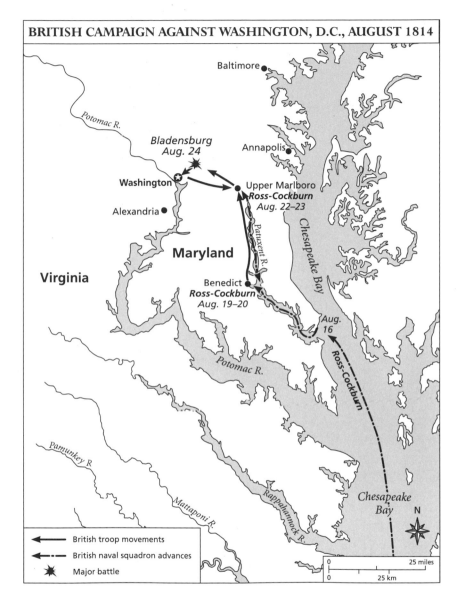

BRITISH CAMPAIGN AGAINST WASHINGTON, D.C., AUGUST 1814

destination, they literally collapsed in an open field near the Navy Yard and went to sleep. When they awoke on the morning of August 24, their orders were "to march back to Bladensburg." The Americans would, after all, make a stand there.

The first part of the battle began at 1:30 P.M. The British opened the attack by storming the Bladensburg bridge across the Potomac. They were driven back by American rifle fire and a two-gun battery. The British reformed their ranks and went forward again. This time they were aided by a weapon the Americans had not seen or even heard of before. It was the Congreve rocket, invented by British artillery officer Sir William Congreve. The rocket consisted of a tube of sheet iron filled with gunpowder set off by a fuse. Congreve based his invention on a missile developed by an Indian prince named Haider Ali, who in turn adapted a similar device invented by the Chinese.

The Congreve rocket was extremely inaccurate. Even Rear Admiral Cockburn admitted that "The bloody things couldn't hit the Tower of London at point-blank range." But it made an appalling noise as it flew over the American lines trailing long streamers of smoke. The American cavalry horses and artillery mules promptly stampeded—and were immediately followed by the American militiamen, most of whom had never before been in battle. Terrified by what they thought were comets, they dropped their guns and ran for their lives. Their flight later became known as "the Bladensburg Races."

But the Battle of Bladensburg was not over. Earlier that day, Commodore Joshua Barney had stormed into President Madison's office, demanding to know why General Winder had not given him and his seamen fighting orders. "These are the precious few fighting men in the whole damned army," the commodore roared. When Secretary of the Navy William Jones suggested that Barney take on the job of protecting the Navy Yard, the commodore became even more incensed. "By God, sir," he shouted, "this is thimble-headed stupidity. I am not going to let my five hundred seamen do a job that any damned corporal in the army could do with five private soldiers. I'll harpoon one of these fish-faced officers first." Finally, it was agreed that Barney, his men, and his cannons—three 18-pounders and two 12-pounders—should proceed to Bladensburg.

"A large part of his men were tall, strapping Negroes," Madison's freedman servant Paul Jennings later reported. "Mr. Madison asked Com. Barney if his Negroes would not run on the approach of the British. 'No, sir,' said Barney, 'they don't know how to run; they will die by their guns first.'"

So Barney and his seadogs headed for Bladensburg, pulling the naval guns—each of which weighed over two tons—by means of harnesses about their shoulders. When they reached their destination, Barney deployed his forces on top of a hill. In addition to the flotillamen, this second line of Americans included militia from Maryland and the District of Columbia. Barney's troops were in the center, with the other Americans to his left and right.

It was now about 2:00 P.M. The first three British assaults were thrown back with considerable damage to British forces. Subaltern Gleig, who was wounded in the thigh, later wrote that the musket fire from Barney's men was the heaviest he had ever experienced. He felt "as though [I] were in a hailstorm, with the shells of the big guns serving as frequent lightning bolts." The flotillamen repulsed the last British charge by a countercharge of their own, which they accompanied with a blood-curdling yell that would later be used by Confederate soldiers in the Civil War.

If only some of the other American troops had held equally fast, most military strategists believe, then Barney's resistance would have forced the British to make a full retreat. But the other Americans did not hold fast, and Barney's force was too small to protect its flanks. The British shifted

Dolley Madison rescued a number of historically important items, such as the famous painting of George Washington by artist Gilbert Stuart, just before the arrival of the British army. *(National Archives, Still Pictures Branch, NWDNS-148-GW-936)*

The burning of Washington, D.C. *(National Archives, Still Pictures Branch, NWDNS-148-GW-478)*

from frontal assaults to flanking attacks from both right and left. By 4:00 P.M. it was all over, at an estimated cost of 600 British casualties (200 killed, 400 wounded) and 100 American casualties (40 killed, 60 wounded). Those seadogs who were still alive retreated, and Barney himself—with a

bullet wound in the hip—was taken prisoner by the British after he refused to leave the field of battle. The road to Washington lay open.

When the British entered the nation's capital toward nightfall on August 24, they found it practically deserted. Most of the civilian population had fled, as had most government officials. At three o'clock that afternoon, Dolley Madison, the president's wife, had abandoned the President's House (now known as the White House) after rescuing a portrait of George Washington by Gilbert Stuart. It had been necessary for her personal servant, French John Siousa, to chop the frame apart with a hatchet in order to remove the canvas.

The redcoats entered "Jemmy's Palace," as they called the President's House, about eleven o'clock that night. They found the dining room table spread for dinner, "which many of us speedily consumed," Capt. Harry Smith reported, ". . . and drank some very good wine also." When they were finished, they set fire to the building, which the Madisons had elegantly redecorated a few years before. The redcoats burned everything—furniture, draperies, linens, books, pictures, papers, food, wines, and family possessions. All that remained were "unroofed naked walls, cracked, defaced and blackened."

The rest of official Washington met a similar fate. The British set fire to the Capitol (which also housed the Supreme Court and the Library of

Congress), the Treasury building, the War Department building, the Navy building, the Post Office Department building, and the State Department building. As Subaltern Gleig noted, "Nothing could be seen except heaps of smoking ruins." Only the Patent Bureau escaped unharmed when its chief, Dr. William Thornton, told the British that "Patents are not the property of the Government, but of the inventors." Fortunately, a heavy thunderstorm that drenched the capital just before dawn kept the fires from destroying the entire city. About eight o'clock that evening, August 25, the British left Washington for their next objective: Baltimore.

News of the burning of the capital shocked the United States. "The blush of shame, and of rage, tinges the cheek while we say that Washington has been in the hands of the enemy," stated the *Richmond Enquirer.* The Winchester, Virginia, *Gazette* attacked government leaders in the bitterest of terms. "Poor, contemptible, pitiful, dastardly wretches! Their heads would be but a poor price for the degradation into which

The White House

THE WHITE HOUSE, ORIGINALLY KNOWN AS THE PRESIdent's House, was the first public structure built in Washington, D.C. It was designed by an Irish architect from South Carolina named James Hoban. The President's House, unlike other buildings in the capital, was made of light gray sandstone rather than wood or plain brick. Its first occupant was John Adams, who moved in when only six rooms were usable. His wife, Abigail, would hang her laundry in one of the unfinished rooms because, as she complained, there was "not the least fence, yard, or other convenience" outdoors.

Thomas Jefferson had the building's slate roof replaced with a rainproof iron roof. He also had the outside of the building whitewashed to prevent mildew.

The President's House was rebuilt after the War of 1812. At that time, its exterior walls were painted white to cover the stains caused by the fire the British had set during the war. Additional rooms were added over the years. The name White House became official in 1902, when President Theodore Roosevelt had it imprinted on his stationery.

"THE DARKEST DAY"

The President's House as it appeared in 1807. *(Library of Congress)*

they have plunged our bleeding country." The *United States Gazette* of Philadelphia urged Madison and his associates to resign. If not, the paper insisted, "They must be constitutionally impeached and driven with scorn and execration from the seats which they have dishonored and polluted."

How had the United States come to such a pass, its capital burned and its government publicly despised? For that matter, why was the United States at war with Great Britain? Most Americans were of British descent. They spoke English, followed English theories of government to a great extent, and traded extensively with Great Britain. Those who could afford to copied English styles of furniture, clothing, and art and sent their oldest sons to England for a college education. Yet less than three decades after the United States won its independence from Great Britain, Americans and Englishmen were once again locked in combat. What had brought about this new military conflict between the two nations?

2

"FREE TRADE AND SAILORS' RIGHTS"

Wars are rarely, if ever, fought for one reason alone. Rather, a host of economic, political, and sometimes social and cultural reasons impel nations and their citizens to resort to armed conflict. The war that was officially declared on June 18, 1812, was the culmination of a series of events dating back to 1783. These events involved not only the United States and Great Britain but France, four North African states, and several American Indian nations as well.

The end of the Revolutionary War in 1783 brought problems as well as independence to the new United States. For one thing, the Treaty of Paris that ended the war did not clearly define the border between the new nation and the British colony of Canada. As a result, each side claimed some of the same land—especially in Maine—and there were frequent border skirmishes. Also, under the treaty terms, the British were to evacuate Detroit, Niagara, Sandusky, and four other fortified posts south of the Great Lakes. But the British were in no hurry to do so. They were accustomed to using the forts as centers for their fur trade with the Indians and were reluctant to disturb this highly lucrative business. Also, many Indians were military allies of the British, who regarded their support as essential in keeping control of Canada. Accordingly, as more and more Americans moved westward into the Ohio Valley, Kentucky, and other frontier areas, the British supplied the Indians with arms and ammunition and reportedly encouraged them to attack the settlers.

In 1787 Arthur St. Clair was appointed the first governor of America's Northwest Territory (the present-day states of Ohio, Indiana, Illinois,

In 1794, Anthony Wayne led American troops to victory over a confederation of Indian nations in the Battle of Fallen Timbers. The resulting Treaty of Greenville, negotiated by Wayne, ceded present-day Ohio and the surrounding lands to the United States. *(National Archives, Still Pictures Branch, NWDNS-148-GW-468)*

Michigan, Wisconsin, and part of Minnesota). Four years later, he launched a campaign against the Indians in the territory. But his 2,000 troops were untrained and poorly equipped, and many deserted soon after they joined up. The remaining Americans were ambushed by the Indians along the banks of the Wabash River (near present-day Fort Wayne, Indiana). Some 900 were killed, while the rest fled for their lives.

Three years later, in 1794, the tables were turned. An American force led by Maj. Gen. "Mad Anthony" Wayne—so called because of his reckless courage—defeated the Indians at a place called Fallen Timbers (near present-day Toledo). Among the Indians who fought that day was a tall, 25-year-old Shawnee known as Tecumseh. Americans were to hear his name many times in the future.

That same year, President George Washington sent Chief Justice John Jay to England to negotiate a new treaty. The Treaty of London, known in the United States as Jay's Treaty, was ratified by Congress in 1795. Under its terms, Great Britain again agreed to evacuate its forts south of the Great Lakes. By 1796 it did so. Although British fur traders were still allowed to carry on their trade on the American side of the border, Jay's

Great Britain turned over Fort Niagara to the United States in 1796 under the terms of Jay's Treaty. *(Sempronius Stretton / National Archives of Canada / G18775)*

Treaty managed to avert war. But it did not end America's problems with the British any more than the Treaty of Greenville (Ohio), also signed in 1795 in the aftermath of Fallen Timbers, ended the troubles between the white settlers and the Indians in the Northwest Territory.

The young nation was also threatened on the high seas. One area of particular risk was the western Mediterranean. For centuries, pirates from the North African states of Morocco, Algeria, Tunis, and Tripoli which bordered the southwestern shores of the Mediterranean—known as the Barbary Coast—had been seizing ships and seamen and holding them for ransom. Then, in the late 1600s, the English made a pact with the bey, or ruler, of Tunis. Under the terms of this "nonaggression treaty," the English agreed to pay "protection money." In exchange for a yearly tribute, the bey promised not to seize any English ships, crews, or passengers.

Before the Revolutionary War, American ships enjoyed the protection of the British flag. Following independence, however, they were no longer protected. The Mediterranean trade had been important to the

American economy prior to the war, and American merchants were eager once more to export such products as wheat, flour, rice, and dried fish. But what price should the new nation pay for such trade? Should it pay tribute? Or should it use force against the pirates?

President George Washington turned to his secretary of state, Thomas Jefferson, for advice. Jefferson considered himself a man of peace. Moreover, he was not inclined to cede much power to a federal government. But the idea that Americans would be subjected to these pirates' criminal acts—held for ransom, chained as rowers on the bey's war galleys, or sold as slaves on the auction block—triggered a ferocious response in Jefferson. In December 1790 he appeared before the U.S. Senate and presented the alternatives of "war, tribute, and ransom." The Senate promptly voted to set up a naval force. However, it added a provision: "It will be proper to resort to the same *as soon as public finances permit.*" The reality was that the new nation could not yet afford a navy.

In 1793 a fresh assault on American shipping by Barbary pirates, with the resultant capture of 11 ships and almost 100 seamen, forced Congress to consider the issue again. Arguments raged. Some said the United States could not afford to fight both the Indians and the pirates. An army could be disbanded, but once naval ships were built, they were a continuing

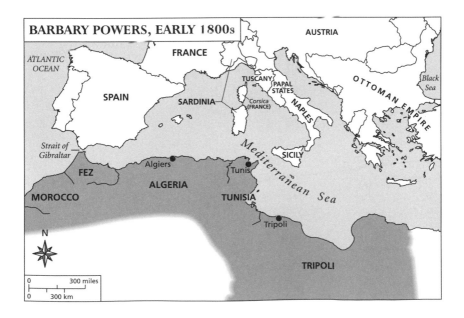

Thomas Jefferson,
third president of
the United States,
saw the need for
the use of military
force to regain U.S.
freedom on the seas.
(Library of Congress)

expense. Others argued that if nothing were done, insurance rates on merchant ships would continue to rise. So, too, would the amount of tribute expected. Some politicians observed that building naval ships would provide jobs, always a persuasive point.

On March 27, 1794, President Washington signed the bill authorizing the establishment of the U.S. Navy. However, construction of the six frigates that were to comprise the fleet took longer than expected. The first ship, the USS *United States,* would not hit the water until May 10, 1797. Accordingly, when Algeria offered to negotiate a peace treaty in 1795, the United States did not have any ships ready for warfare. Congress therefore agreed to pay a lump sum of $642,000 to ransom American prisoners, as well as an annual tribute of $21,600 worth of arms—guns, powder, and shot.

A year later, the United States signed a similar treaty with Tripoli. However, Tripoli's ruler, known as a bashaw or pasha, was not satisfied and in 1801 he demanded additional tribute. The United States refused. After all, it was paying 20 percent of its annual revenues to the Barbary

States! The bashaw then declared war on the United States. But by this time Jefferson was president. Five days after his inauguration, he convened his cabinet and made it clear that he wanted to use force against the bashaw. An advocate of strict interpretation of the Constitution, Jefferson knew he needed congressional approval to declare war—and Congress was not in session. Nevertheless, the president was convinced that he had the power to send American ships to the Mediterranean under the constitutional mandate "to protect American commerce."

In June 1801, an American fleet of four frigates sailed for the Mediterranean. The frigates carried members of the U.S. Marine Corps, which

The U.S. Marine Corps

THE U.S. MARINE CORPS HAD ITS BEGINNINGS DURING the American Revolution when the Continental Congress, in 1775, organized two federal battalions of marines. The corps disappeared at the end of the war but was recreated by the U.S. Congress in 1798. Since then, marines have fought in all U.S. wars.

They were very active in the War of 1812, taking part in all of America's major naval victories. Capt. John Gamble fought so well that he became the only marine officer in American history to receive command of a naval ship. It was a captured British warship. Marines also played an important role in the Battle of New Orleans in 1815, when Andrew Jackson's army defeated the British. Marines were the first units sent into Afghanistan in the early phase of the war against the Taliban in 2001.

In addition to fighting in wars, marines have taken part in various actions to protect American interests. For example, they landed in China to defend foreign legations that were besieged in Beijing during the Boxer Rebellion of 1900, and they landed in Panama to keep the isthmus open between 1885 and 1903.

Members of the U.S. Marine Corps specialize in assault operations that are launched from ships. The corps is a branch of the U.S. Navy in the Department of Defense. Nevertheless, it operates as a separate service with its own aircraft, artillery, and tanks.

Marines are sometimes called leathernecks because in the past they used to wear leather collars to protect their necks. The Marine Corps' official colors are red and gold. Its motto is *Semper Fidelis* ("Always Faithful").

The USS *Philadelphia* was stranded off the coast of Tripoli and captured by Tripolitan sailors on October 31, 1803. *(National Archives, Still Pictures Branch, NWDNS-19-N-13264)*

had been authorized by Congress in 1798. The marines' battle duty was to lay down a barrage of rifle fire and grenades to prevent the Barbary pirates from swarming aboard the ships. The exploits of these Americans are commemorated in the Marine Corps song by the words "to the shores of Tripoli."

One of the heroes of the Tripoli campaign, which lasted four years (1801–05), was a dashing young naval lieutenant named Stephen Decatur. In October 1803, the American frigate *Philadelphia* had run aground on a reef close to the harbor of Tripoli and had been seized intact by the Tripolitans. The bashaw had had the ship's crew stripped down to their underwear, imprisoned in an old stone warehouse, and set to forced labor. The ship's officers received better quarters and better treatment but were nonetheless held captive.

On December 23, 1803, Decatur captured the *Mastico,* one of the Tunisian ships involved in the taking of the *Philadelphia.* Decatur renamed the ship the *Intrepid* and crammed it with 75 sailors and marines. He then disguised the *Intrepid* as a Maltese ship and, in a brilliant

20-minute action, sailed into the harbor at Tripoli, where he threw grappling ropes on the *Philadelphia* and set it ablaze, thus rendering it useless to the enemy.

Decatur was one of the last men to jump clear before the ropes were cut. He managed to get the *Intrepid* away without the loss of a single American life.

Decatur's daring action won the United States the respect of European nations. The raid also helped conclude the Tripoli campaign. In 1805, the United States agreed to ransom American prisoners, while Tripoli promised to stop seizing American ships. However, the United States continued to pay tribute to the other Barbary States—albeit at rates lower than other nations paid—until 1815. In that year, an American fleet under Decatur would finally bring an end to both piracy and payments.

The Barbary pirates were not alone in harassing American ships and seamen. The British were also bent on interfering with American commerce on the high seas. When the War of Independence ended, Britain

Stephen Decatur's daring rescue of American sailors in Tripoli made him a popular hero of the war. *(Library of Congress)*

tried to stifle American economic competition. It prohibited American ships from trading with itself or its colonies. In response, American merchants either smuggled goods into British ports that were not patrolled by the Royal Navy, or else sold goods to countries that then resold them to Britain and its colonies. Naturally, such actions roused the anger of the British ruling and merchant classes.

Another reason for British interference with American shipping was political. In 1789, the same year Washington became the first president of the United States, the French Revolution erupted. For 10 years thereafter, France experienced a series of weak governments and radical leaders. Then, in 1799, a young military genius named Napoleon Bonaparte seized power. Napoleon was determined both to conquer Europe and to destroy Great Britain's superiority on the high seas. By 1802, he had achieved much of his first goal. However, Great Britain still controlled the Atlantic.

In 1803 the conflict between France and Britain—which had stopped the previous year—heated up again. Americans saw the renewed conflict as a chance to expand their European markets. With French and English farmers leaving the land to serve in their country's army and navy, it was a golden opportunity for Americans to export the production of their own soil and industry.

France and Britain looked at the situation differently. Each wanted to prevent the other from obtaining supplies, and each claimed the right to seize neutral ships bound for the other's ports. This left the United States in a quandary. If it traded with Britain, it risked losing ships and cargoes to France. If it traded with France, it risked losing them to Britain. Still, the profits from foreign trade were so high that American ships continued to sail to Europe and sell to both sides. In fact, American overseas commerce increased more than sevenfold between 1803 and 1807, from $13.6 million to $107 million.

There was one thing, however, that made British interference with American shipping seem worse than French interference. That was the British declaration that they had the right of "search and seizure." To a British captain, this meant not only that he could stop a ship flying the Stars and Stripes and examine its cargo, he could also search for sailors who had deserted British ships.

Desertion was a major problem for the Royal Navy, and small wonder: The work was hard, the food poor, and the pay only seven dollars a month as compared with the American pay rate of $30 a month. In addition,

British ships used flogging as a disciplinary measure. One sailor described the experience this way:

> The boatswain starts you by a stroke on the back with his cat-o'-nine-tails [a length of tarred, knotted rope]. Every man then strikes you as hard and as fast as he can. "You have to go round the deck three times in this manner. It is in vain for you to cry, scream, jump, roll, for you must bear it. Finally you look like a piece of raw beef from your neck to your waist. You are taken down to the cockpit, and there have salt brine rubbed on your back. If you are so fortunate as to get over this, you must go to work again.

Deserters from the Royal Navy soon learned that they could put themselves under American protection by jumping ship at an American port and taking out naturalization papers. British captains, however, usually refused to honor such papers: "Once an Englishman, always an Englishman." Some British captains went even further. They refused to recognize America's independence and adopted the practice of impressing, or forcing, even American-born seamen into their service. During Jefferson's first administration, for example, more than 1,500 Yankees were grabbed from American merchant ships and made to serve on King George III's naval vessels.

Both Jefferson and his secretary of state, James Madison, tried negotiating with Britain to stop the search and seizure operations, but without success. The situation worsened in 1806 when shots fired by a British frigate killed a Yankee sailor in American waters. Protest riots broke out in New York, and a few American newspapers even called for a declaration of war.

Another incident, in 1807, created additional tension, and this time there was enough bloodshed to arouse the American public as a whole. In the spring of that year, several British seamen slipped ashore at Norfolk and enlisted on the newly commissioned American frigate *Chesapeake*. One of these sailors, named Jenkin Ratford, in a celebratory mood, shouted insults at some British officers who had likewise gone ashore. The officers reported the incident to British authorities, who demanded the return of the deserters. The Americans refused.

On June 21, the British frigate *Leopard* arrived off the coast of Norfolk with orders to search for deserters should it meet the *Chesapeake*. The next day, as the *Chesapeake* was cruising just outside the three-mile limit off Virginia, it was hailed by the *Leopard,* which demanded the right to examine its crew and impress deserters. Although his guns were not yet in firing order, the *Chesapeake's* captain, Comm. James Barron, refused to obey. How dare the British try to take seamen from a naval vessel! It was bad enough taking them from merchant ships.

At that point, Capt. Salisbury Humphreys of the *Leopard* opened fire. For 10 minutes, 50 British guns pounded the defenseless *Chesapeake.* With three men killed and 18 wounded, including himself, Barron was forced to yield. He ordered the firing of a single shot in honor of his flag—then submitted to a search. The crew was lined up, and four men were seized as alleged deserters. One was Jenkin Ratford. The other three were "an American Negro, an Indian, and a native of Maryland."

News of the attack on the *Chesapeake* created headlines in newspapers throughout the United States. In villages and towns everywhere, people discussed and debated what they considered the latest outrage against the honor and rights of their country. Congressmen spoke up in protest, and war fever swept the nation.

Jefferson, however, preferred a different approach, one he called "peaceful coercion." He demanded that Britain return the seamen taken from the *Chesapeake* and pay money to the wounded and the families of those killed. He told British warships to leave American territorial waters. And in December 1807, he persuaded Congress to pass the Embargo Act.

Under the Embargo Act, American ships were forbidden to sail from a U.S. port to any foreign port. American exports were prohibited. And a long list of British manufacturers were refused entrance to American markets. In essence, the nation's foreign trade was to come to a standstill.

What Jefferson hoped for was a cooling-off period so that the United States could maintain Washington's foreign policy of noninvolvement in European conflicts. The president knew the United States was the largest consumer of British manufactured goods. It was also the world's largest neutral shipper. Jefferson hoped that economic pressure on the warring powers of Britain and France would bring them to their senses as far as interference with American shipping was concerned. Jefferson also hoped that the embargo would stop the importation of luxury goods and encourage the growth of American industries.

Things did not work out that way. The embargo actually proved profitable for both the English and the French. The English turned to the Spanish colonies for whatever imports they needed. They also took over

Reacting to the Embargo

THOMAS JEFFERSON'S EMBARGO OF 1807 INFURIATED many people. Some referred to it as "dambargo"; other opponents turned the word around and called it "O-grab-me" because it pinched their pocketbooks. Still other people sang or recited the following ballad, which first appeared in the *Herald* of Newburyport, Massachusetts.

> Our ships all in motion once whitened the ocean,
> They sailed and returned with a cargo.
> Now doomed to decay, they are fallen a prey
> To Jefferson—worms—and Embargo.

Before the embargo, Newburyport had been a prosperous seaport. Farm and forest products floated down the Merrimack River and were shipped across the Atlantic. Manufactured goods were imported from Europe. Whaling ships made use of the harbor, and local shipyards turned out schooners and seagoing sloops.

After the embargo was imposed, trade came to a standstill. Most people were thrown out of work. Many went hungry, and thievery became common. Young men left Newburyport to ship aboard foreign vessels. The town lost 100 voters in just one year. Even after the embargo was repealed, Newburyport was unable to recover its former prosperity.

the international trade the Americans had given up. The French thought the embargo was the next best thing to an outright American declaration of war against Great Britain. And the Canadians did a healthy business in smuggled goods. The only people who suffered from the embargo were Americans.

In the Northeast, much dependent on trade, shipping, and fishing, the embargo was a terrible hardship. Ships rotted at the docks and thousands of seamen lost their livelihood. As the Newburyport, Massachusetts, *Herald* reported: "Our wharves have now the stillness of the grave—indeed, nothing flourishes on them but vegetation." In the South and the West, farmers and planters faced huge surpluses, declining prices, and bankruptcies. The price of cotton, for example, which had reached 51 cents a pound in 1805, plummeted to 24 cents a pound by

1808. Tobacco, wheat, and other farm products were similarly affected. Overall, American imports dropped from $60 million in 1807 to less than $13 million in 1808, while exports tumbled from $107 million to $22 million.

The loudest protests came from New England, where town meetings were held and local courts refused to enforce the federal law. But southern and western congressmen objected also. After 14 months, Jefferson acknowledged that the embargo was a failure. So Congress repealed the Embargo Act and substituted the Non-Intercourse Act, which allowed American ships to trade with all nations except Great Britain and France.

In 1809 Jefferson was succeeded in office by James Madison. A short, round-faced, soft-spoken man, Madison had earned his political reputation as one of the nation's Founding Fathers. He had been instrumental in the adoption of the Constitution and the Bill of Rights. He had served as Jefferson's secretary of state, and rumor had it that it was Madison who had suggested the ill-fated embargo to the former president.

Like Jefferson, Madison preferred negotiation to war. Accordingly, in 1810 he convinced Congress to pass a new law by which the United States promised that if either Britain or France lifted its restrictions on American shipping, Americans would resume the embargo against the other nation. France agreed to do so and the United States promptly forbade all trade with Britain. Napoleon, however, did not keep his side of the bargain, reasoning that the United States was too weak militarily to do anything about it. Instead, France continued to seize and scuttle American ships.

In the meantime, however, the American embargo against Britain began to take effect. Why now, when it had failed before? One historian would later explain it this way:

> The winter of 1811–12 was the bitterest that the English people experienced between the Great Plague [of 1665] and 1940–41. . . . [A French blockade] had now closed all western Europe except Portugal to British goods. American non-intercourse shut off the only important market still open except Russia. . . . A crop failure drove up the price of wheat, warehouses were crammed with goods for which there was no market, factories were closing, workmen rioting. Deputations from the manufacturing cities besought Parliament to repeal [its laws against American shipping], . . . hoping to recover their American market.

"FREE TRADE AND SAILORS' RIGHTS"

James Madison,
father of the
Constitution and
president of the
United States
throughout the war
(Library of Congress)

Finally, on June 16, 1812, Parliament suspended British laws against American shipping. If only there had been a transatlantic "hot line" to convey the news to the American people, many historians believe that the War of 1812 would not have happened. Instead, on June 18, unaware of what had taken place two days earlier in London, Congress issued a declaration of war.

In his message recommending the action, President Madison stressed "Free Trade and Sailors' Rights" as the leading cause of the conflict. Yet New England, which owned about three-fourths of America's merchant fleet and was home to most American seamen, bitterly opposed the war. It was the congressmen from other sections of the new United States, especially those from west of the Allegheny Mountains, who favored it. Both at the time and in the decades since, the War of 1812 is often portrayed as one fought primarily over the United States's maritime rights and relations. In fact, only by looking closely at Americans' dealings with the inhabitants of the western territories—both Native Americans and British—can the true causes of the war be understood.

3

WARRIORS
AND WAR HAWKS

"One of those uncommon geniuses which spring up occasionally to produce revolutions and overturn the established order of things." Those words of a future president of the United States, William Henry Harrison, were used to describe Tekamthi, the great leader of the Shawnee Indian nation. English speakers, finding the lisping sound unseemly, called him Tecumseh.

Tecumseh was born in 1768 into a culture that was undergoing great change as a result of the arrival of Europeans in North America. The Shawnee still depended upon hunting, food gathering, and the planting of small gardens for their food supply. But they now used the guns, tools, and utensils of the white settlers. Their clothing was no longer made solely from deerskins. Much of it was made of the Europeans' cloth of linen or wool.

Nor were the Shawnee as self-sufficient as they had been in the past. They were now part of the colonial economic system, a system based on the fur trade, which stretched over the Appalachians and across the Atlantic. The Indians trapped beaver, mink, muskrat, and raccoon and exchanged the fur pelts with the British for trade goods. When the price of pelts fell, or the animal population declined, the Shawnee standard of living suffered.

Westward-moving pioneers created yet another problem for the Shawnee. The pioneers who settled in the Northwest Territory always wanted more land because existing farming techniques (employing little or no fertilizer) exhausted the fertility of the soil after several years.

Also, many of the settlers believed that the United States was destined to keep expanding until it controlled the entire continent of North America. The Treaty of Greenville, which followed the Battle of Fallen Timbers in 1795, forced the Shawnee to give up most of their traditional homeland. They were now limited to the northwest quarter of Ohio, at the so-called Greenville line. By 1800, they could already see white settlers pouring into southern Ohio. And many of the newcomers were illegally setting up squatter cabins north of the Greenville line.

The Long Knives, as Indians called white men because of the weapons they carried, were also destroying the deer herds that were the Shawnee's main source of food and clothing. As William Henry Harrison, then

Tecumseh, powerful Shawnee leader and orator, fought to defend his people's land and heritage. *(Library of Congress)*

governor of the Indiana Territory, acknowledged in 1802, "One white hunter will destroy more game than five of the common Indians—the latter generally contenting himself with a sufficiency for present subsistence—while the other eager after game hunt for the skin of the animal alone." Harrison may have understood the problem, but he failed to offer any remedy for the Indians' concerns.

There were additional problems. Europeans had introduced new diseases—such as measles, whooping cough, smallpox, and influenza—to the American continent. Even more devastating was the new social disease the whites brought, namely, alcoholism. Whiskey was one of the goods that traders sold to the Indians in exchange for furs. By the late 1700s, drunken warriors were a common sight, and women too were becoming addicted to the potent liquid. Shawnee chiefs pleaded for the use of government troops to stop the traders from peddling whiskey, but their requests were unanswered.

Indian family life suffered not only from new diseases and alcoholism but also from direct attacks. White hunters would enter isolated or unattended Indian camps and steal horses and other items that they could sell later. They seized Indian children between the ages of two and six and smuggled them across the Ohio River, where they were either adopted by white settlers or apprenticed to tradesmen. The Indians tried to defend themselves, and lives were lost on both sides. In some instances, Indians who entered trading posts were murdered in cold blood.

Crimes against the Indians went unpunished. It was impossible to obtain a conviction from a pioneer jury when, as Harrison admitted, frontiersmen "consider the murdering of the Indians in the highest degree meritorious." On the other hand, if an Indian stole a horse or other property, the government would take the cost of the stolen property out of the annual payments it gave the Indians for their land.

The situation of the Indians was becoming desperate. Their land, their means of livelihood, and their culture were fast disappearing. The times demanded strong leadership. The man who tried to fill that role was Tecumseh.

Tecumseh's background and physical presence did much to enhance his image. His family had traditionally produced chiefs, and he had the appearance and bearing of a leader. At five feet 10 inches, he was taller than the average Shawnee warrior and was reportedly muscular, a good hunter, and a skillful fighter. But his greatest asset was probably his talent

White settlers attacking Indian villages were rarely brought to justice for their actions. *(Library of Congress)*

in oratory. When he spoke, his eloquence and clarity riveted the attention of Indian and white audiences alike.

Tecumseh's message was simple. The only way in which the Indian nations could survive was by forming a single, strong alliance and resisting the white man's encroachment on their land. "The Great Spirit gave this great land to his red children," Tecumseh argued. "He placed the whites on the other side of the big water. They were not contented with their own, but came to take ours from us. They have driven us from the sea to the lakes. We can go no further."

It was Tecumseh's contention that no single Indian chief, or even any single Indian nation, had the right to sell land to the whites. "[The land] never was divided, but belongs to all for the use of each. . . . Sell our land? Why not sell the air, the clouds, and the great sea?" Tecumseh reminded his Indian listeners that one Indian nation after another had disappeared. "Where today are the Pequots? Where are the Narragansetts, the Mohawks, the Pocanets and many other once powerful tribes of our people? They have vanished before the avarice and oppression of the white man, as snow before a summer sun." The time had come to stand firm.

Tecumseh's political leadership was reinforced by the religious leadership of his brother, Lalawethika. Until 1805, the half-blind Lalawethika had been considered nothing more than an alcoholic braggart. But one night, after awakening from a trance, he claimed that he had been transformed by the Master of Life (the term used to describe the Indians' Supreme Being). From that day on, he announced, his name would be Tenskwatawa, "the Open Door," and he would devote his life to persuading other Indians to give up liquor and to turn away from the ways of the whites and return to those of their ancestors.

Tenskwatawa, whom Americans called the Prophet, and Tecumseh worked hard during the early 1800s. Tecumseh visited one Indian nation after another, from the Menominee in Wisconsin to the Osage in Missouri to the Creek in Alabama. Everywhere his message was the same: the Indian nations had to stand together or they would be unable to prevent white expansion and their own annihilation. For his part, in 1805 Tenskwatawa established a village on the site of the fort in Ohio where the 1795 Treaty of Greenville had been signed. Here Indians from nearby nations came to hear his sermons against drink and against any contact with whites except for trade.

The activities of Tecumseh and the Prophet alarmed Harrison, especially after the two brothers in 1808 set up a new village near the juncture of the Wabash and Tippecanoe Rivers, west of the Greenville line. The new village, which was named Prophetstown, put the Shawnee farther from white settlers and American military expeditions and closer to the Indian nations of Illinois and Michigan, many of whose members were supporters of the brothers. Equally important, in the woods surrounding the new settlement game was still plentiful, while fish abounded in the nearby rivers. At Prophetstown, the Shawnee could more easily follow their traditional way of life.

Harrison's attitude was typical of that held by many Americans. "Is one of the fairest portions of the globe to remain in a state of nature, the haunt of a few wretched savages, when it seems destined, by the Creator, to give support to a large population, and to be the seat of civilization, of science, and of true religion?" And he proceeded to put his beliefs into action.

In 1809 Harrison rounded up a few chiefs of the Miami, Delaware (Lenni Lenape), and Potawatomi Indian nations, got them drunk, and succeeded in persuading them to give up 3 million acres of land in exchange for $7,000 worth of trade goods. This acquisition meant that the Shawnee no longer had any hunting grounds.

The Treaty of Fort Wayne infuriated and emboldened Tecumseh. He begged Harrison to cancel the treaty, but the governor refused. Tecumseh thereupon declared the treaty null and void—and asked the British in Canada for arms and supplies. Then he set off for Kentucky, Tennessee, and Alabama to once again exhort the Indians there. This time, he called on them not merely to resist but to destroy the whites.

> Burn their dwellings. Destroy their stock. The red people own the country.... War now. War forever. War upon the living. War upon the dead; dig up their corpses from the grave; our country must give no rest to a white man's bones.

Harrison struck first. On September 26, 1811, he led an army of about 1,100 men north from Vincennes. At a site where Terre Haute stands today, he ordered the building of a stockade that he immodestly named Fort Harrison. He then continued northward and on November 6 crossed the Wabash and set up camp on the opposite side of Tippecanoe Creek from Prophetstown.

Shawnee warriors rush the American troops at the Battle of Tippecanoe. (*Library of Congress*)

That night, both sides began preparations for an attack. Harrison posted sentries around the camp and alerted his men to sleep with their weapons. At the same time, the Prophet—ignoring Tecumseh's instructions not to fight until reinforcements arrived—met with about 600 armed followers. At midnight, the Indians surrounded the American encampment. They waited quietly for four hours and then began moving forward. But before they could pierce the enemy lines, an alert American sentry fired a warning shot, and the battle was joined.

Ordinarily, the Indians would have advanced gradually, taking cover behind trees and large rocks before making the next move forward. But the night before, the Prophet had told his followers that he had put a spell on the Americans that weakened their ability to defend themselves. The spell had also made the Indian warriors invulnerable to enemy bullets. So instead of following their usual tactics, the Indians ran straight at the American line—and were promptly mowed down.

Propelled by his great popularity as "the hero of Tippecanoe," William Henry Harrison was elected president of the United States in 1840. *(Library of Congress)*

Dying in Office

WILLIAM HENRY HARRISON—POPULARLY KNOWN AS "Old Tippecanoe"—should have known better. After all, he had been a medical student in his college days. Nevertheless, he paid no attention to the weather on March 4, 1841, when he was inaugurated as the United States's ninth president. It was bitterly cold that day, yet Harrison refused to put on a coat. Not only that, his inaugural address, delivered outdoors, lasted almost two hours, the longest inaugural address in American history. The result was that the new president caught a cold. The cold turned into pneumonia, and Harrison died 31 days later. Harrison was the nation's first chief executive to die in office.

Less than 10 years later, President Zachary Taylor succumbed to cholera. Abraham Lincoln was assassinated, as were James Garfield and William McKinley. Warren G. Harding died suddenly from either a stroke or a heart attack. Franklin Delano Roosevelt suffered a brain hemorrhage. John F. Kennedy was assassinated. In all, four presidents died from illness and another four were killed. Ronald Reagan was shot but recovered from his wound.

After three Indian attacks, Harrison mounted a counterattack. He forced the Indians, who by this time had run out of arrows and ammunition, to retreat across the marshy prairie. He then entered Prophetstown and burned it to the ground, destroying all the Indians' supplies. American casualties were 62 dead and 126 wounded; Indian casualties were about the same.

To Harrison, the Battle of Tippecanoe was a great victory. It certainly bolstered his personal ambitions. His name was carried far and wide in the newspapers of the day, and in his successful run for the presidency in 1840, he would refer to the battle in his campaign slogan, "Tippecanoe and Tyler Too."

For white settlers in Indiana and Illinois, however, the Battle of Tippecanoe meant increased danger. The Indians forced to flee from Prophetstown were extremely bitter at their defeat, and they translated their bitterness into a series of raids all along the frontier. Whole families of whites were wiped out, and many pioneer farmers fled from the

Many Americans suspected that the Indians were allied with the British, as shown in this cartoon of the period. *(Library of Congress)*

territory. At the same time, Tecumseh worked to rebuild his shattered confederacy with the help of food and arms from the British.

The increased turmoil in the West reinforced a political change that was occurring in the United States. The change showed itself most clearly

they'll in a dreadful Fright,
Refuge to the Woods in Flight;
ders then will quickly shake,
wrongs shall restitution make.

in the new 12th Congress, which was elected in 1810. The face of this Congress was quite different from the previous one. It was not the youth of the new members, although most of them were in their twenties and thirties, nor was it their numbers, although they made up about half of the House of Representatives. Rather, it was their attitude. The newcomers had not been old enough to serve in the Revolution or help in the founding of the new nation. But they were immensely proud of being Americans and determined both to preserve their country and not to suffer any insults to their flag. They deeply resented British attacks on American shipping and British impressment of American seamen. They also remembered the British-Indian alliance that had existed during the Revolution and felt that a similar alliance was in the making. In addition, many of them had personal reasons for hating Indians.

The victory at Tippecanoe galvanized these new congressmen. They demanded that the United States declare war on Britain and invade Canada. "We shall drive the British from our continent," asserted Felix Grundy, a product of the Tennessee frontier who had lost three brothers in Indian raids. "They will no longer have an opportunity of intriguing with our Indian neighbors."

Grundy was joined in his demands for war by two other representatives from frontier areas, Henry Clay of Kentucky and John C. Calhoun

Henry Clay, Speaker of the House of Representatives, favored war with Great Britain as a means of annexing Canada. *(National Archives, Still Pictures Branch, NWDNS-111-B-4201)*

of upland South Carolina. Clay was a strong supporter of American expansion. He felt that as the country's population grew, it would inevitably require more land—Illinois, western Tennessee, Florida (which was then owned by Spain), and the "fertile, wooded peninsula of Upper Canada between Lakes Huron, Erie, and Ontario." Calhoun's grandmother had been scalped by the Cherokee, and he had grown up on stories of his father's exploits against the Indians and the British. It was his speeches about the *Leopard*'s murderous attack on the *Chesapeake* that brought him before the public and swept him into Congress on the stirring issue of national honor. Grundy, Clay, Calhoun, and others with similar sentiments were dubbed "War Hawks."

On November 11, 1811, the War Hawks elected Henry Clay as the Speaker of the House on the first ballot. He promptly proceeded to turn a rather perfunctory administrative post into a position of party leadership. He enforced strict rules of order and, using his power of appointment, packed all the important committees with War Hawks. The most important committee was the Foreign Affairs Committee, to which Clay appointed both Calhoun and Grundy. The committee also included Maryland representative Philip Barton Key, who had a son named Francis Scott Key.

Within weeks, the Foreign Affairs Committee hammered out a strong set of resolutions calling for increases in both the army and the navy. In the meantime, the War Hawks in Congress took every opportunity to denounce even the smallest British insult. Finally, President Madison realized that national sentiment had shifted decisively and that the time had come to fight. He sent a note to Great Britain demanding that it lift all restrictions against American shipping. When no answer was forthcoming by June 18, he asked Congress to declare war.

The United States was now about to go to war against the world's most powerful nation. The political and military events that led up to this declaration of war have been examined. But wars are not fought only by military and political leaders; they are fought by citizens. How were the people of the United States really living in the summer of 1812? And how had their way of life changed since the nation's formal founding only some three decades before?

4

THE UNITED STATES ON THE EVE OF WAR

The United States that declared war against Great Britain in 1812 was quite different from the nation that had won its independence 29 years before. For one thing, the United States had almost doubled in size. In 1793 it contained about 870,000 square miles and was bounded on the north by Canada and on the west by the Mississippi River. The land to the south, which would later become Florida and the coastal strip of Alabama and Mississippi, belonged to Spain. Then, in 1803, the French emperor Napoleon Bonaparte sold the United States the Louisiana Territory—roughly the land drained by the western tributaries of the Mississippi. As a result of this real estate transaction, which cost just $15 million, or 3 cents an acre, the United States now contained approximately 1.7 million square miles, while its western boundary lay more or less along the Rocky Mountains and the Red River of Texas.

In addition to expanding geographically, the United States had grown in terms of population. In 1783 the country contained fewer than 4 million inhabitants. By 1812 there were more than 7.2 million Americans. Their ethnic heritage, however, remained almost unchanged. About half were men and women of English descent. About one-sixth were African Americans, the vast majority of whom were still slaves. Another one-sixth were Celtic Americans: Scotch-Irish, Scottish, and Welsh. The remaining one-sixth of the population consisted mostly of Germans and Dutch, with a few citizens of French and Swedish descent thrown in. About 100,000 American Indians were concentrated on tribal territories

THE UNITED STATES ON THE EVE OF WAR

Mills powered by water became the centers of early industrial towns during the first part of the 19th century. *(Library of Congress)*

in the northeastern and southeastern parts of the country. Others were scattered throughout the forests, plains, and hills of the north-central and western parts of the country.

Although some urbanization had taken place since 1783, Americans in 1812 were still a predominantly rural people. More than four out of five farmed. Unlike their counterparts in Europe—where farmers lived in closely settled communities from which they departed in the morning to work the land and to which they returned at night—most farmers in the United States lived apart from each other, on their own farmsteads. Northern farmers were usually in sight of their nearest neighbors, but most southern and western farmers were not. A major exception was on southern plantations, where slave cabins were set close together in single or double rows behind the planter's "great house."

As a result of this farming pattern, rural communities in the the United States were mostly commercial rather than agricultural villages. They were inhabited chiefly by shopkeepers, artisans, and lawyers, and farmers would come to town from miles around to trade and to find

Almanacs

ALMANACS WERE THE MOST POPULAR PUBLICATIONS in the United States during the early 1800s. They were small pamphlets that contained predictions about the weather for the coming year, advice on household problems, medical hints, adventure stories, and jokes. But the main reason farmers read them was for their agricultural information.

Although farmers worked every day with plants and animals, they did not know much about what actually affected crops and herds. What they considered to be most significant was the phases of the moon. For example, one was supposed to plant certain crops at the dark of the moon and other crops when the moon was almost full. One planted radishes "downward at the decrease of the moon, for they tapered downwards." One slaughtered hogs when the December moon was waxing. Otherwise "the pork would shrink and wither away in the barrel."

services. But here and there, primarily in the North, a different kind of rural community was beginning to emerge. It was situated near a stream and was characterized by a water-powered factory building around which were clustered the boardinghouses inhabited by the mill workers, with a general store and a church nearby. By the 1840s, the North would contain hundreds of mill towns in which workers turned out such manufactured products as cotton and woolen textiles, chairs, brooms, farm implements, hats, shoes, and guns.

Of the nation's urban inhabitants around 1812 (those living in communities of 2,500 or more), most were concentrated along the coast. The six major seaports were New York (population 96,400), Philadelphia (53,700), Baltimore (45,500), Boston (33,000), Charleston (24,700), and New Orleans (17,200). All six cities were small in area. Buildings stood cheek by jowl, while the narrow, manure-littered streets were jammed with people walking and goods being moved in horsedrawn wagons. Since most urban buildings were made of wood rather than brick, fires were common, a situation worsened by the lack of public fire departments. Salaried police forces and sanitation workers were likewise nonexistent, which tended to encourage a high crime rate and frequent outbreaks of such diseases as dysentery, measles, tuberculosis, typhoid fever, and yellow fever. Only smallpox had been almost eradicated as a result of the use of vaccination after 1796.

Yet despite the crowding, noise, dirt, crime, and disease, more and more Americans were finding cities exciting places in which to live. They offered tremendous opportunities for making money in trade. And they were the incubators of new fashions, furnishing styles, books, songs, dances, and other forms of culture.

American farmers in 1812 were limited in what they could do by muscle power. Mills for grinding grain and sawing timber were powered by falling water, as were the textile mills that were beginning to rise in New England. But everything else depended on human effort assisted by animals. The animals used varied from region to region. Northern farmers usually worked their land with oxen, which were surefooted in rocky areas. Farmers in the West, where farms were larger and the terrain flatter, preferred speedier and more maneuverable horses. Southerners expanded their animal work force with mules, which were slower than horses but had more endurance.

The most common farming tool was the hoe, followed by the axe, the plow, and the scythe. The only important machine that American farmers used was the cotton gin, which had been developed in 1793 by Eli Whitney with help from Catherine Littlefield Greene. The gin enabled a worker to remove the seeds from 50 pounds of short-staple cotton in one day as compared with cleaning one pound by hand. Later improvements multiplied the machine's productivity 60 times.

The invention of the cotton gin sparked numerous changes in the South's economy. "King Cotton" replaced tobacco, rice, and sugarcane as the staple crop. Cotton production soared from 10,000 bales in 1793 to more than 175,000 bales in 1812. (It was to reach almost half a million bales by 1830—and continue rising.) As cotton cultivation used up the land in Maryland, Virginia, and the Carolinas, large numbers of farmers began pushing westward into Alabama, Mississippi, and even Texas, which was then part of Mexico. At the same time, southern planters began placing increased emphasis on breeding slaves as fast as possible in order to meet the heightened demand for labor. Thus, slavery, which had been gradually dying out in the South, revived.

Many farmers in 1812 were also "mechanics"—that is, they combined the raising of crops and livestock with the making of goods by hand. They made barrels, bricks, furniture, horseshoes, pots, and dozens of

Money and Barter

IN THE EARLY 1800S, THE MONEY USED IN THE UNITED States consisted mostly of gold and silver coins. However, the coins were not necessarily minted by the federal government. In fact, the most popular coins were those minted in Mexico: silver dollars, halves, quarters, eighths, and sixteenths. As well as coins from England and France, there were also the so-called rix-dollars from the Netherlands and kopecks from Russia. Whenever people used any foreign-minted coins, they had to convert their value into U.S. dollars and cents.

Needless to say, using money was a complicated matter in the early 1800s. Merchants and city dwellers were accustomed to it. But many rural folk preferred to swap goods and services. For example, a farm woman might bring some butter, eggs, and beeswax to the country store and exchange them for so many yards of dry goods. A farmer might lend a neighbor a horse and wagon to use for two weeks in exchange for a few weeks' pasturing of a cow. This system, known as bartering, is still practiced not only throughout the world but even on many occasions in the United States.

other products used in everyday life. Sometimes they exchanged such goods with their neighbors; sometimes they sold their goods to country merchants, who in turn sold them to the public at large.

Mechanics in the cities were specialists who worked full-time at their craft. Many of these crafts duplicated those performed in rural areas, but some were more or less restricted to urban areas. In general, printers, bookbinders, silversmiths, clockmakers, and milliners were found only in the cities. Because mechanics worked according to the job rather than the hour, their work schedule was very uneven, with a period of relaxation succeeded by a period of "desperate industry." Mechanics usually learned their skills by serving an apprenticeship.

Other occupations that Americans followed in 1812 were fishing, lumbering, and fur trading. Like farmers to their fields, most fishermen went out each day in their own boats and brought back their catch for their families. The only fishing industry was whaling, in which the company that owned the ship provided crew members with gear and provisions and paid them with a share of the catch. Lumbering, like fishing, was organized on an individual basis. Loggers working on their own supplied timber to widely scattered and independent sawmills.

Only the fur trade was developing into a full-fledged industry. This was primarily because of the activities of John Jacob Astor. A leading fur merchant in New York City, Astor realized that the Louisiana Purchase had changed the nature of the fur trade. Individual trappers and traders could no longer exploit the fur resources of the West because of the distances involved and the hostility of the Plains Indians. So in 1808 Astor organized the American Fur Company and in 1810 sent out two expeditions to set up a trading post at the mouth of the Columbia River in Oregon. Astor would be forced to sell the post to a Canadian company during the War of 1812. But as soon as the war was over, he would persuade Congress to pass a law forbidding foreigners (meaning the British) from taking part in the American fur trade. By the 1820s the American Fur Company would hold a monopoly of the nation's fur trade and Astor would become America's first millionaire.

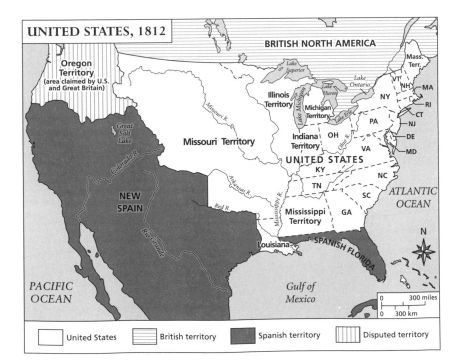

As with farming, fishing, lumbering, and the crafts, manufacturing in 1812 was performed primarily on an individual basis. But it was in this area that the most significant change in the American economy was under way.

The change dated from 1789, when 21-year-old Samuel Slater migrated from England to the United States. Great Britain, which had been industrializing for more than 50 years, had banned the emigration of mechanics and the export of machine designs. Slater, however, memorized the plans for a textile mill, pretended to be a farmer, and came to this country to seek his fortune. In 1791 he opened the first successful full-time factory in the United States, a cotton-spinning plant in Pawtucket, Rhode Island. By 1810 more than 100 textile mills, employing principally women and children earning less than a dollar a week, were operating throughout New England. During the 1820s and 1830s the textile industry was to become the largest industry in the nation.

Shortly after Slater opened his factory, another major step toward industrialization occurred. In 1798 Eli Whitney opened a firearms factory near New Haven, Connecticut. The factory utilized the principle of interchangeable parts, which had two major effects on manufacturing. First, it made it possible to turn out a great many products in a short period of time. Second, it was no longer necessary to employ mechanics: unskilled workers would do. By the 1830s, mass production and the factory system would be on their way to dominating the American economy.

In 1812 most Americans—whether country or city dwellers—lived and worked in households where they shared their sleeping quarters and their meals. The average household contained six persons, but about four out of 10 Americans lived in even larger households, with eight, nine, 10, or more members. Household members did not necessarily belong to the same family. In fact, the typical household of the period included not just parents and their children but also nonrelated workers. Thus, if the head of the household worked a farm, his household included the hired hands. If the head of the household ran a bookbinding shop, his household included the shop's journeymen and apprentices. It was almost unheard of to live alone. People who did so were considered eccentric at best, mad at worst.

Households often fluctuated in size. A widower or a widow would move in with a married brother or sister. A younger brother might spend a year or two learning a trade before striking out on his own. A

Both in town and on the frontier, much of the life of an American house-hold in the early 19th century centered around the fireplace. This hearth scene was photographed at the Joseph Gilpin house, near Chadd's Ford, Delaware County, Pennsylvania. *(Library of Congress)*

sister of marriageable age might pay an extended visit in order to meet a potential husband.

Most households were crammed with children, for the birthrate was high. The average white American couple in 1812 could expect to have seven or eight children, one of whom would die by the age of one and another of whom would die by the age of 21. Although the birthrate among African Americans was similar, their infant and childhood mortality rates were much higher. About one out of three died by the age of one, and only about half survived to adulthood.

Yet by 1812 a trend toward smaller families was already under way. It began in the longest-settled eastern part of the United States, where both the economy and the society were fairly stable and where women were better educated than elsewhere. As a result, parents were having no more than four or five children. Over the years, the trend would spread to other parts of the country.

Men's Clothing and Hairstyles

MEN'S CLOTHING FASHIONS AND HAIRSTYLES BEGAN to change dramatically in the early 1800s. Before the turn of the century, men wore knee breeches, long coats with broad tails, and hats with low crowns and wide brims. After the turn of the century, knee breeches gave way to long pants, coats became short and close-fitting, and hats—known as "stovepipes"—had high crowns with narrow brims. One historian described the longer pants and shorter coats as "an embellished version of the working costume of sailors and laborers." In other words, the new style of men's clothes reflected the fact that the United States was developing into a commercial and industrial society.

Before 1800, most American men dressed in homespun, that is, linen or wool or a combination of the two that was produced at home. Clothes made of homespun were easy to spot. Their fabrics were coarse and their outlines were baggy. Wealthier men had their clothes made out of woolen broadcloth, fine linen, and imported cotton and silk. These fitted the wearers' bodies closely.

After 1800, as textile manufacturing developed in the United States, people gave up homespun and substituted factory-made cloth of cotton and wool. By 1840, ready-made clothing appeared, and the former difference between clothing made at home and that made by "city tailors" began to disappear.

Men's hairstyles changed along with their clothes. Before 1800, members of the upper class either wore elaborate wigs or, at the very least, powdered their hair. Farmers and workingmen usually wore their hair in a long braid, which they tied with eel skins or black ribbons. After 1800, largely as a result of the example of Thomas Jefferson, wigs and powder were no longer considered fashionable. Instead, men of both the upper and lower class wore their hair cut short.

The houses in which Americans lived varied according to region and to their owner's wealth. The great majority, however, were very small compared to present-day dwellings.

In the West, houses were mostly one-room log cabins about eight feet by 12 feet. In the North, the average wood farmhouse measured about 20 feet by 24 feet and contained two or three rooms. A cellar served to store food during the hot summers, while the privy stood outdoors, often in the front yard. A well-to-do farmer lived in a larger house, usually with two stories and six or seven rooms. The difference between rich and poor in northern cities was similarly great. Rich people lived in two-story houses of brick or stone with 10 to a dozen rooms, while poor people lived in one-room wood huts that measured about 14 feet by 17 feet. Dwellings in the South were likewise diverse. Wealthy plantation owners lived in two-story mansions similar to those in the North. The average southern farmer lived in a house that measured about 16 feet by 24 feet, with the kitchen as a separate structure. Slave quarters were smaller; one or two families inhabited a log hut about 10 feet square.

Yet houses, like rural communities, were beginning to change as the economy changed. In such commercial centers as Baltimore and Philadelphia, for example, street after street was filling up with connected brick row houses. By eliminating side walls and rising three or four stories, row houses made good use of the narrow city lots. Likewise, by the 1820s industrial centers such as Lowell, Massachusetts, were building brick boardinghouses for workers that resembled factories in size and shape.

Home furnishings, like houses, varied according to the owner's wealth. Just about every family owned several beds. Rich people slept on feather beds, poor people on straw ticks. The customary practice was three to a bed, except for the head of the household and his wife. Not until the 1820s would travelers be able to ask innkeepers for "one person, one bed." Just about every family also owned a table and at least three wood chairs. Candlesticks, however, were rare, while window curtains and carpets were almost nonexistent.

Most Americans used wood-burning fireplaces for warmth as well as for cooking purposes. Unfortunately, since houses were not insulated, the fireplaces were effective just within a small area. Only the houses of German settlers, who brought cast-iron stoves with them from their homeland, were comfortable in cold weather.

Yet furnishings, too, were beginning to change. Here and there parlors boasted upholstered sofas and chairs, whale oil lamps shone with the power of 10 candles each, and housewives were cooking on stoves instead of kitchen fireplaces. In addition, effects of the Industrial Revolution were starting to appear and would intensify over the decades to follow. By 1830 power looms would be weaving enough carpets for one out of five homes. Machine-made textiles would enable families to put curtains on their windows. Machine printing would bring the price of

Deadly Diseases

DURING THE WAR OF 1812, MORE AMERICAN SOLDIERS and sailors died from disease than were killed by the enemy. Many Americans succumbed to pneumonia brought about by cold weather and the lack of warm clothing. Others died from infections that developed after operations. Surgeons in those days did not know about sterilizing equipment to kill germs.

Disease, in fact, was widespread among all Americans in the early 1800s. The first year of life was the riskiest. The main cause of death was an infection of the lungs or intestines, such as pneumonia, typhoid, or dysentery. Doctors at that time had no idea how these and other diseases were transmitted. They knew nothing about bacteria or viruses or the role of mosquitoes in carrying disease. One result of high infant mortality was that many parents delayed naming their children until they were at least six or seven months old.

Once past their first birthday, the main threats to children were chickenpox, measles, mumps, scarlet fever, and whooping cough. These diseases often ravaged whole families at a time. From their mid-teens on, farm boys—who worked with heavy loads and sharp-edged tools—were particularly susceptible to accidents that resulted in open wounds. These wounds often became infected, which in turn led either to "mortification"—gangrene—or "blood poisoning"—septicemia. Because antibiotics had not yet been discovered, gangrenous arms and legs had to be amputated, while septicemia was usually fatal.

The two major diseases of adulthood were malaria, commonly known as "intermittent fever" or "the ague," and pulmonary tuberculosis, or "consumption." Malaria seldom resulted in death. Instead, victims of the disease suffered periodic shaking fits. Pulmonary tuberculosis, however, was probably the most common cause of death in the United States before the Civil War.

wallpaper down to an affordable level. And the development of mass-produced clocks after 1806 would enable one out of two Americans to have a clock in the house by 1830.

Perhaps the outstanding characteristic of American domestic life was the abundance of food. One result was that most Americans were two or three inches taller than most Europeans.

The two food staples of 1812 were corn and what one traveler referred to as "the eternal pork." Families in the dairying North were able to add butter, cheese, and beef to their diet, while families in the more heavily forested South and West relied on venison, possum, and other game for much of their meat. Hard apple cider was a favorite drink of northerners, except for Germans, who favored beer. Southerners and westerners were more partial to whiskey. (The temperance movement would not have any noticeable effect until the 1820s, when many families would begin replacing beer and liquor at the dining table with water.) All Americans, however, were drinking more coffee and tea each year. They were also using increasing amounts of sugar to sweeten their drinks and to improve the taste of such bland foods as cornmeal mush.

Other aspects of the American diet were likewise changing. People everywhere were eating more vegetables, such as cabbages, onions, turnips, and squash. These not only added variety to meals but also served as protection against scurvy and other vitamin deficiency diseases. Americans were also eating potatoes instead of bread—"Irish," or white, potatoes in the North and yams, or sweet potatoes, in the South.

Although most Americans worked hard, they did not neglect the lighter side of life. By 1812 horse racing had moved northward from the South, where it had been popular since colonial times, and almost every large town in the United States boasted a racecourse on its outskirts. People usually wagered with each other on the outcome of the races. They also gambled at billiards, cards, dice, dogfights and cock-fights, and wrestling matches. Although gambling was illegal in most of the country, the laws against it were seldom enforced.

The most common form of recreation, though, was the practice of music. People sang everywhere—in church, at work, at weddings and other public events, and for home entertainment.

Singing in church took one of two forms. In the cities, congregations usually listened quietly as well-trained choirs, accompanied by organs, performed from written texts and tunes. In rural areas, the entire congregation sang without instrumental accompaniment. Since money for hymn books was scarce, worshipers memorized a few popular tunes. But although they tried to memorize the words of the hymns as well, in most instances they followed the practice of "lining out"—that is, a leader would read aloud one or two lines from a hymn book and the congregation would sing the lines in response.

However, in church music as in other areas, change was under way. Beginning about 1800, evangelical Protestantism became popular among black slaves in the South. By the time the War of 1812 broke out, slaves were composing their own powerful, rhythmic songs called spirituals—according to Jack Larkin in *The Reshaping of Everyday Life,* "a sort of prayer in rhyme, in which the same words occurred again and again." Gradually, spirituals were to shape the words and melodies of white religious music.

Black slaves in the South were also the most common singers of work songs, which they used to mark the rhythm of their labor. As historian Jack Larkin has explained:

> Songs helped black rowers time their strokes, woodsmen mark their blows as they felled trees, or cotton pickers, cane cutters, and rice harvesters keep pace with their work. "We would pick cotton and sing, pick and sing all day," wrote a black autobiographer.

Americans enjoyed playing and singing popular tunes, many of which had political or military themes. *(Library of Congress)*

Dancing was a favorite pastime for Americans rich and poor. *(Library of Congress)*

Weddings, sleighing parties, and barn raisings were occasions for singing old ballads from England and newer broadside songs. The ballads, like "Barbara Allen" and "Chevy Chase," dealt with such topics as tragic death, violence, and the blighting of love. Part of an oral tradition, they were passed on from one singer to another.

Broadside songs, which became increasingly popular after 1800, originated in print form. The words were printed on a broadside, or single sheet of paper, and sold for a penny apiece. Whoever bought the sheet simply fitted the words to a popular tune. At least one out of three broadside songs dealt with political and military events, such as the American Revolution. Others dealt with events of everyday life, examples being "The Lawyer Outwitted" and "The Old Maid's Last Prayer." And still others portrayed such calamities as "The Dreadful Hurricane at New Orleans," to say nothing of murders, piracy, and Indian warfare.

Music for home entertainment was popularly known as parlor music because it was usually performed in the parlors of homes. By 1812, at least among well-to-do urban families, this increasingly meant the music was played on the new pianofortes by daughters. Such parlor music served a dual purpose in addition to entertainment. It enabled young girls to display their music-making talents before prospective suitors.

And it enabled their parents to show off a musical instrument that cost as much as half a year's wages for a carpenter.

While pianofortes were played mostly by women, other musical instruments were more or less reserved for men. Both informal dances and formal balls were accompanied by fiddlers, many of them black. State militias performed their martial exercises to the sound of fifes and drums. And slaves often accompanied their songs with self-made banjos and "bones"—percussion instruments consisting of a pair of animal jawbones or shankbones.

Americans enjoyed music but they valued education even more. They wanted their children to be able to read, write, and calculate. As a result, most white youngsters between five and 15 years of age attended school for several months a year, and about three out of four adult white males were literate. The literacy rate among white females was lower, however, and among slaves was practically nonexistent. But although most Americans could read, they did not read a great deal. Books were expensive and there was little light available for reading at night. As a result, most book-owning families owned only a Bible and the year's almanac. As for newspapers, although many communities had a weekly paper, these were usually delivered not to private homes but to taverns and stores, where they were read aloud to groups of people.

Nevertheless, although the United States still depended on Great Britain for most books, an American literature was beginning to develop. By 1793 enough Americans had written poems to allow for publication of an anthology entitled *American Poems, Selected and Original.* The year 1809 saw the publication of Washington Irving's *History of New York,* a burlesque of early Dutch settlers. Irving's *Sketch Book,* which appeared in 1819, would create two well-known American folk figures: Rip Van Winkle and Ichabod Crane.

When the War of 1812 broke out, there were no railroads in the United States (steam-powered railroad service would not appear until 1831), so people traveled long distances overland by stagecoaches or on horseback. The stagecoaches were flat-bottomed vehicles without springs or braces, which made riding in them extremely uncomfortable. Although they were designed to seat only 12 passengers on backless benches, drivers usually managed to crowd a few more people on board.

Not only were the stagecoaches uncomfortable but the roads—even the post roads that linked Boston to New York and New York to Philadel-

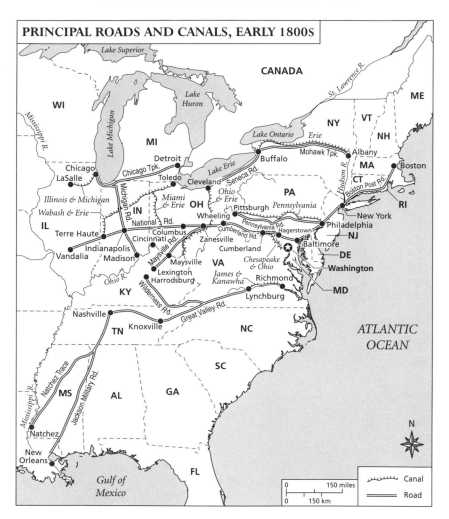

PRINCIPAL ROADS AND CANALS, EARLY 1800S

phia and Baltimore—were little more than wagon ruts. An Irish visitor to the United States named Isaac Weld wrote that "The driver frequently had to call to the passengers to lean out of the carriage, first at one side, then the other, to prevent it from oversetting in the deep ruts. 'Now, gentlemen, to the right,' on which the passengers all stretched their bodies half way out of the carriage to balance it on that side. 'Now, gentlemen, to the left,' and so on." Despite such precautions, "upsettings" were common, caused by anything from boulders and potholes to broken axles and runaway horses.

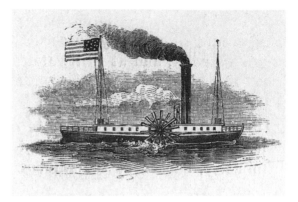

Fulton's steamboat made its first trip to Albany on August 18, 1807. *(Pictorial Field-book of the Revolution)*

Goods as well as people moved over the nation's roads. Some goods were carried in horse-drawn freight wagons, and a six-horse team pulling a four-ton load could cover 25 or 30 miles a day. During wintertime, farmers in New England sledded their butter and cheese to market on horseback. Animal traffic on the roads (one way from farms to livestock markets and butchers' stalls) varied depending on the time of year. Sheep began moving to market after the wool-shearing in July, while cattle and pigs choked the roads between October and December. An animal drover could cover about 13 miles a day.

However, changes in overland transportation were beginning to appear. In 1811 the federal government let contracts for the building of the National Road, although actual construction would not get under way until the War of 1812 was over. Starting in Cumberland, Maryland, the road at first went across the Appalachian Mountains to the Ohio River city of Wheeling, Virginia (now West Virginia). Later, the road was extended all the way to St. Louis, Missouri. The National Road eventually enabled hundreds of thousands of Americans to move westward. It was the first of many "internal improvements" financed by the federal government that would help to tie the different regions of the United States together.

Travel by water was faster, easier, and cheaper than travel by land. Individuals commonly used birchbark canoes. Families and livestock on the Ohio and other western rivers floated downstream on flatboats or on roofed barges called "Kentucky arks." These were only used once, being broken up and sold for lumber when they reached their destination.

Yet here, too, a major change was under way. In 1807 Robert Fulton launched the first commercially successful steamboat on American waters. Within a decade after the *Clermont* chugged its way up the Hudson River, steamboats were carrying farm products on the Ohio and Mississippi Rivers, especially sugar and cotton toward New Orleans. And the development of the steamboat soon led to the expansion of the nation's system of canals. By 1825 the Erie Canal (363 miles from Buffalo to Albany) would form an important part of an all-water system that carried grain from Midwest farmers to New York City and on to international markets.

But before the United States could take advantage of the worldwide economic opportunities that were opening up, it had to deal with the major obstacle of Great Britain. Rivalry in transportation and trade between Great Britain and its former colony was a major cause of the War of 1812.

5
"GO MARCH TO CANADA!"

Washington Irving, who was just beginning to emerge as America's first successful native-born author, had several times described President James Madison in unflattering terms. To Irving, the president was a man with "his forehead full of wrinkles, a face which has the appearance of a midnight lamp." It was true that Madison was short and unprepossessing in appearance. Yet on June 1, 1812, when he finally sent his war message to Congress, there were good reasons for him to have a wrinkled brow.

For one thing, the nation's armed forces were small in number and ill-prepared for combat. Earlier in the year Congress had authorized the acceptance of 50,000 volunteers for a year's service. But by the time war was declared, fewer than 5,000 men had signed up. In all, the U.S. Army contained perhaps 7,000 troops. That meant the state militias would have to fight, too. But, as would emerge on several occasions, the governors of the various states were reluctant to allow their militiamen to fight outside their own state's borders. And there would be times when the commanding officers of the militia would simply refuse orders to commit their men, even when the regular troops were threatened.

The armaments and supplies for both militiamen and regular troops would also be at best of uncertain quality throughout the war. After the Revolutionary War, most Americans had not seen much purpose in maintaining a first-class army, so there were precious few new arms of any kind. Many of the heavy artillery pieces that would be used by the Americans in the War of 1812, in fact, had been captured from the British

The Musket

FROM THE 1500S TO THE 1800S, THE MOST COMMON weapon used by soldiers was the musket, or flintlock. It was about five feet long and weighed about 10 pounds. Ammunition consisted of cartridges, or lead balls, that weighed about 1 1/2 ounces apiece. Each cartridge was wrapped in paper and carried in a cartridge pouch that dangled from a soldier's waist or shoulders. A soldier also carried gunpowder in a horn.

To load his musket, a soldier poured some gunpowder down the front of the barrel into the pan of the firing mechanism. He tore the paper off a cartridge with his teeth and rammed the cartridge down the barrel by means of a long steel ramrod. Then he aimed the musket and pulled the trigger. This caused the hammer of the firing mechanism to fall. A piece of flint on the hammer produced a spark, and the spark in turn ignited the powder charge. The resulting explosion sent the cartridge flying out of the barrel.

Muskets took about half a minute to load and were not particularly accurate. They were, however, quite deadly when fired by hundreds of infantrymen standing shoulder to shoulder.

Until the 1800s, muskets were expensive. They were made by hand, and each musket took about one week to make. Moreover, no two muskets were exactly alike, so it was not possible to "cannibalize" parts. A barrel from one gun, for example, could not be used to replace a broken barrel on another gun.

After the use of interchangeable parts was adopted in the early 1800s, the situation changed. Now a single factory could turn out thousands of guns a year, and for a much lower price. By 1815, the federal government had made interchangeable parts a requirement in all its contracts with gun manufacturers.

during the Revolution. As for guns, most of the American troops would be armed with the old muzzle-loaded muskets of the kind used in the Revolutionary War. Militiamen, furthermore, all tended to carry their own favorite weapons, so there could be little standardization when it came to spare parts and ammunition.

All other supplies—especially food—conformed to the same low standard. When food was not in short supply it was close to inedible. As

The legendary character of "Uncle Sam" was created during the war of 1812.
(Library of Congress)

it happened, it was during the War of 1812 that "Uncle Sam" emerged as a symbol of the government because of food supplies. Samuel "Uncle Sam" Wilson, a meat provisioner and inspector working for the army around Troy, New York, would stamp the purchased containers of salted meat with a "U.S." Allegedly those opposed to the war began to claim that the letters stood for "Uncle Sam"—a way of mocking the government. (The name first appeared in print in a Troy newspaper in 1813.) As the usage spread, "Uncle Sam" became a symbol of the United States itself. (The first cartoons with Uncle Sam in his traditional costume did not appear until the 1830s.)

The militiamen, of course, were little more than weekend soldiers—men who spent at most a few hours each week practicing some simple drills and perhaps taking target practice. To make matters worse, even the regular soldiers were poorly trained and without battle experience. Many were not really interested in a military career. They had simply signed up for one year to see what army life was like. As soon as their enlistment term was over, they would take off for home—even if a major battle was set for the following day.

Most of the army's officers were equally disappointing and unreliable. Winfield Scott, one of the few American army officers to emerge from the War of 1812 as a hero, described the situation this way: "The old officers [those who had fought in the Revolutionary War] had very generally slunk into either sloth, ignorance, or habits of intemperate drinking." An example of such an officer was Maj. Gen. Henry Dearborn, who would be given command of the campaign against Canada. He was so stiff in the joints and out of touch with his surroundings that he was commonly known as "Granny."

The War Department was likewise inadequate and unprepared. Congress had refused to fund any enlargement of the department, so the entire staff consisted of Secretary William Eustis and eight clerks.

In addition, the country was sharply divided over the war. Not a single member of the Federalist Party in Congress voted in favor. New England in particular vehemently opposed the conflict. In Hartford, Connecticut, flags were lowered to half staff when news of the war's declaration was received, and the state vowed not to send its men to fight. Massachusetts and Rhode Island announced that their citizens would not fight, either. (In fact, as the war went on, New England volunteers provided 19 regiments to the regular army.)

Only the West and the South were truly enthusiastic. There, people marched in parades and drums beat out a call for recruits. "The hour of national vengeance has arrived," frontiersman Andrew Jackson told his Tennessee militia. They were going to fight "for the establishment of our national character . . . for the protection of our maritime citizens impressed on board British ships of war . . . to seek some indemnity for past injuries, some security against future aggression by the conquest of all the British dominions upon the continent of North America."

And in that last phrase was summed up the true motive and goal of the war's most vocal supporters: to conquer Canada. It was not just the bordering land and lakes that they coveted. Many Americans sincerely believed that only by conquering Canada would the British once and for all be removed as a threat to the United States. And only by conquering Canada would the Indians be removed as a threat on the western frontier. As John Randolph, the maverick representative from

Roanoke, Virginia, described the "cant of patriotism" he so despised: "Like the whippoorwill, but one monotonous tone—Canada! Canada! Canada!"

There was another reason why Jackson and so many other Americans believed that conquering Canada was the way to win the war. The United States was ill equipped to challenge Great Britain at sea. The American fleet numbered only a half dozen frigates, three sloops, seven brigs, and about 70 gunboats (these last too small and light to be of much use). In contrast, the British navy contained hundreds of warships with cannons capable of attacking both American ships and seaports. An American victory at sea seemed impossible.

A victory on land, however, was a different matter. Americans assumed that Britain's long struggle with France had drained Britain's resources and that Canada would thus have few soldiers and supplies with which to fight Americans. The most populated part of Canada, moreover, was the province of Quebec, where most of the people were of French descent. How could the British depend on their loyalty? There were the Indians, of course, but General Harrison's victory at Tippecanoe showed that they would be no problem. Two years earlier, Henry Clay had proclaimed to Congress, "The conquest of Canada is in your power. I trust I shall not be deemed presumptious when I state that I verily believe that the militia of Kentucky are alone competent to place Montreal and Upper Canada at your feet." Taking Canada would be a breeze— or so the War Hawks promised. Reality proved otherwise.

Unlike the United States, Canada had two capable men heading its armed forces. Both were experienced soldiers, although with very different ideas as to how the war should be run.

Lt. Gen. Sir George Prevost was the governor of Lower Canada (the area north of Vermont that included Montreal) as well as commander in chief of all provinces. Prevost, 44 years of age, was a prudent man, more diplomat than soldier. He was very much aware that his troops were short of rifles and that the lengthy Canadian coastline would be difficult to protect with the limited forces at his command. His plan was to fight a defensive war. In a message to his subordinate, Isaac Brock, Prevost argued that the numbers did not "justify offensive operations being taken, unless they were solely calculated to strengthen a defensive attitude."

General Brock was the governor of Upper Canada (the area north of Lake Huron, Lake Erie, and Lake Ontario). A muscular, handsome man in his early forties who stood six feet two inches tall, Brock prided himself on being hard as nails. He made his own interpretation of Prevost's order.

For the previous five years, ever since the *Chesapeake* incident in 1807, Brock had been preparing for war. He put himself in the boots of his enemy and anticipated what the enemy's plan might be. The natural

Sir George Prevost, governor in chief of Canada, planned to fight defensively rather than attack the United States. *(Samuel William Reynolds/National Archives of Canada/C-6152)*

place for the Americans to attack Canada was at Montreal, Canada's major city. Taking Montreal would block the St. Lawrence River and prevent the British from sending reinforcements from Quebec. Once British supply lines to Upper Canada were cut, the Americans could move east from Montreal into Lower Canada and capture Quebec. However, if the Indians were to attack the Americans on their left flank as they moved north toward Montreal, the invasion would fail. Brock favored attack rather than defense.

Brock's assumptions about American actions were right on the mark. President Madison put Maj. Gen. Henry "Granny" Dearborn in charge of the attack on Canada—and Dearborn decided to strike at Montreal. His plan called for four invasion forces to cross the border simultaneously. The first force would move from Fort Detroit into the area north of Lake Erie and take care of the western Indians. Two other forces would start out from Sackett's Harbor and Fort Niagara in New York and pin down the British troops north of Lake Ontario so they could not be used to defend Montreal. The last column would march northward along Lake Champlain and the Richelieu River and seize Montreal.

Madison's choice of Dearborn was a poor one. So was Madison's choice of Brig. Gen. William Hull to lead the attack from Fort Detroit. Hull was fat and red-faced from too much eating and drinking. He was almost two decades older than the British generals, and although he, too, had participated bravely in many of the battles of the Revolutionary War, he had never planned a military campaign.

Even before war was officially declared, Hull had gathered 2,000 regulars and militia and begun to march north from Urbana, Ohio, to Fort Detroit, across 200 miles of unbroken wilderness. A contingent of troops was sent ahead to hack their way through the underbrush so that the remaining soldiers and supply wagons could get through. Unfortunately, many of Hull's men caught malaria in the swamp-filled forests, while others dropped dead from exhaustion. In addition, news of the official declaration of war did not reach Hull until July 2 because Secretary of War Eustis sent the message through ordinary mail. In contrast, the British ambassador in Washington sent the news via express rider. So both Prevost and Brock received word of the outbreak of hostilities on June 24 and were ready to act before Hull was.

Hull reached Fort Detroit on July 5, 1812. The word from Eustis was to quickly take Fort Malden, one of a series of British forts that had been built on the Canadian side of Lake Erie after the signing of Jay's Treaty.

Unknown to Hull, a group of Indians had been shadowing the Americans. They had been sent out by their chief, Tecumseh.

Hull made his first attempt to attack Fort Malden on July 12. Much to his chagrin, hundreds of militiamen refused to obey his orders. They had not been recruited to fight on foreign soil, they said. So although Fort Malden was defended by only a few British troops and could have easily been captured, Hull decided to wait.

While Hull dallied, events helped build up a sense of fear among the American troops. A contingent of soldiers had been sent back to escort supplies and militia requested from the governor of Ohio. But before they could reach Detroit, Tecumseh's men attacked, leaving 17 Americans dead and many more wounded. Then news filtered in that Fort Michilimackinac, at the northern tip of the Michigan Territory, had surrendered to the British. Hull now took his troops back to Detroit.

In a surprise attack, British soldiers and fur traders captured Fort Michilimackinac from the Americans in July 1812. *(National Archives of Canada/C-25014)*

Brock had used Hull's delays to advantage. He arranged for a flotilla of ships to transport troops and supplies to reinforce Fort Malden. He also began a series of psychological operations designed to frighten the Americans further. He made sure that a bogus document got into Hull's nervous hands. The document referred to 5,000 Indians ready to descend on Detroit. Then, on August 15, he sent a message to Hull demanding the immediate surrender of Detroit and added, "It is far from my intention to join in a war of extermination, but you must be aware, that the numerous bodies of Indians who have attached themselves to my troops, will be beyond control the moment the contest commences."

Brock's psychological tactics had the desired effect on Hull. During the Revolutionary War, he had seen the work of the Indians—the faces of scalped children, the remains of charred homes, and the mangled bodies of women. His own daughter and grandchildren were among those in Fort Detroit. When Hull was nervous, he would unconsciously stuff his mouth with wads of chewing tobacco until the brown saliva dribbled down over his beard, neckcloth, and vest. Now, watching the saliva dribbling down, Hull's officers realized that the general was falling apart. He was convinced that there were hordes of British in front of him and thousands of Indians behind him. His numbers may not have been accurate, but the British and the Indians were indeed in those positions, awaiting the final word to attack Detroit.

A few days earlier, Brock had met with Tecumseh. Shortly after midnight on August 12, a scout brought the Indian leader to the general's headquarters. Brock was impressed by the stately figure dressed in a simple suit of deerskin, fringed at the seams. Tecumseh was equally impressed by the tall, blue-eyed man wearing a scarlet coat and shiny boots.

The conversation between the two leaders took time, but both men came away pleased at the contact and ready to join forces. Brock wrote later that "a more sagacious and gallant Warrior does not I believe exist. He has the admiration of every one who conversed with him." Tecumseh summed up his feelings about Brock in four words: "This is a *man*." Their relations were further cemented when Tecumseh unrolled a strip of elm bark, removed his knife from his belt, and scratched out an accurate map of Fort Detroit and its surroundings.

When Hull received Brock's demand for surrender on August 15, he panicked. He sent back a reply refusing to surrender but in words that clearly betrayed his uncertainty. Brock thereupon began bombarding the

Brig. Gen. William Hull contemplates the surrender of Fort Detroit to Gen. Isaac Brock, August 16, 1812. *(Felix O.C. Darley / National Archives of Canada / C-8982)*

fort. There was a brief respite during the night that gave Tecumseh the opportunity to surround Detroit from the south side. Then, on the morning of August 16, the British and Indian troops launched an attack.

Most military historians agree that Hull could have repulsed the attack. He had more men and supplies than the enemy did. But it is also probably true that a long siege would have caused starvation and loss of life among the 800 civilians huddled in the fort. So Hull surrendered and at noon of August 16, Brock entered Fort Detroit and proclaimed that the whole Michigan Territory once again belonged to Great Britain. Then the Indians poured in, shooting their guns and seizing the horses. True to his promise to Brock, however, Tecumseh saw to it that no prisoners were molested.

Hull's defeat was received with disbelief and fury throughout the United States. As one American soldier who had been at the fort wrote later: "We could have whipped hell out of the rascals but General Hull has proved himself a traitor and a coward. . . . We were made to submit to the most shameful surrender that ever took place in the world. Our brave Captain Harry James cursed and swore like a pirate, and cried like his heart would break." Two years later, in 1814, Hull was brought before a court-martial. He was found guilty of cowardice and neglect of duty and was sentenced to be shot. However, President Madison spared his life on the grounds of Hull's age and previous military service.

The fall of Fort Detroit was not the only disaster that the United States experienced in August 1812. About a week earlier, Hull had dispatched frontiersman William Wells to Fort Dearborn, on the present site of Chicago. He was to instruct Capt. Nathan Heald, commander of the fort, to evacuate its 100 or so soldiers and civilians as quickly as possible east to Fort Wayne. The garrison contained enough supplies for six months, and the American troops there did not want to leave. But Heald, as a good soldier, agreed to follow the general's orders.

The area around Fort Dearborn was filled with Potawatomi Indians. Believing them to be friendly, Heald gave them all the trade goods from the post store that were not needed for the march to Fort Wayne. Under cover of night, he also dumped all the fort's whiskey into the Chicago River and destroyed surplus weapons and ammunition. Unfortunately, Heald's assessment of the friendliness of the Potawatomi was a gross error. Tecumseh's agents and British traders had done their work well. When the Indians discovered that Heald had destroyed the whiskey and the guns, the two items they most wanted, they were furious.

On August 15, Wells led his party through the stockade door and along a path that would someday be Chicago's famed Michigan Avenue. The Americans were escorted by a column of Potawatomi. Legend has it that Wells, who had lived among the Indians for much of his life, had painted his face with black gunpowder, an Indian sign that he expected death before sundown.

Shortly after the Americans left Fort Dearborn, the Potawatomi escort disappeared into the coastal sand dunes. A mile and a half from the safety of the fort, Wells spotted the Indian ambush. But it was too late. Heald and his men fought furiously with bayonet and musket, but the small force of 57 Americans was overwhelmed by some 500 Indian warriors. Wells himself was killed by the Potawatomi chief Blackbird. The chief then carried out an Indian ritual that paid tribute to Wells's courage: Blackbird cut out Wells's heart and ate it raw.

Most of the American civilians in the party also perished. Children huddled in a wagon were killed and scalped. Some of the soldiers' wives, armed with their husbands' swords, valiantly tried to fight off their attackers and were hacked to pieces. The few civilians who survived became captives of the Indians and were later distributed among villages in the area.

A few months later, the United States suffered yet another defeat. After the surrender of Fort Detroit, Madison replaced Hull with Tippecanoe hero William Henry Harrison. By September 1812, Harrison had assembled an army of some 10,000 men, many of them new recruits from Kentucky and Tennessee. He then set out to retake Fort Detroit. But autumn rains turned the wilderness to mud. So Harrison decided to wait until winter, when the Detroit River would freeze over and he would be able to attack across the ice.

On December 20, Harrison ordered Gen. James Winchester to set up a post at the Maumee Rapids opposite Fort Malden. When Winchester arrived at the rapids, he found two messengers from the village of Frenchtown (near present-day Monroe, Michigan) begging for help. The village lay 40 miles ahead on the Raisin River, and the 33 families living there were under the control of 250 British and Indian troops. After consulting with his officers, Winchester sent an advance party to Frenchtown under the command of two popular officers from Kentucky, Colonels William Lewis and John Allen.

Indian security measures tended to be careless during the frigid winter months, and Lewis and Allen were able to surprise the enemy. The Kentuckians swarmed into Frenchtown and by dusk had driven the British and Indians away. The Kentuckians were ecstatic. After months of cold and hunger, there was cider, whiskey, butter, fresh apples, and the warmth of a house and a fireplace.

When Winchester learned that Frenchtown had been secured, he moved up the rest of his 1,000 men. On the opposite shore, Col. Henry Proctor, the British commander at Fort Malden, was also on the move with 1,200 to 1,400 men, half of them Indians.

At dawn on January 22, 1813, Proctor's forces closed in on Frenchtown. By the end of the day, the Battle of Raisin River was over—and the Americans had lost. Winchester agreed to surrender provided Proctor would protect American prisoners from the Indians. But Proctor was in a hurry to return to Fort Malden before any reinforcements arrived from Harrison. So he left only a small British guard on duty. The Indians fell on the American prisoners with tomahawk and scalping knife.

Between the battle and the massacre, more than 400 Americans died at Frenchtown. Hundreds more, those still able to walk, were marched north by the Indians, never to be heard of again. Harrison learned of the defeat when 30 survivors of Frenchtown limped into his camp. He promptly retreated to the Portage River. When news of the event reached the newspapers, the United States had a new battle cry: "Remember the Raisin!"

The western thrusts into Canada had failed to produce any success. Actions along the central part of the border proved equally dismal. For his first operation in that sector, General "Granny" Dearborn had chosen Stephen Van Rensselaer, a military amateur, to lead an army of 6,000 Americans across the Niagara River with the goal of cutting the portage road between Lake Ontario and Lake Erie. Unfortunately, most of these Americans were militiamen, lacking in both experience and leadership; they also lacked proper food and supplies and were plagued by illness. Opposing the Americans were 1,600 British regulars and 300 Indians under the command of the experienced General Brock.

The Americans' initial target was the high ground overlooking the village of Queenstown. Their first attempt to cross the Niagara River met with failure. On the night of October 10–11, 1812, in a driving downpour, Van Rensselaer's troops slogged their way to a crossing site, only to find that someone—either accidentally or deliberately—had taken the boat that was laden with the oars for all the other boats. Two nights later, on October 12, a second attempt was made. This time, there were not enough boats to transport all the troops, so only 800 men crossed over, while tools and extra ammunition had to be left behind. Commanding these men was 26-year-old Lt. Col. Winfield Scott, who had joined the U.S. Army only four years before.

The Americans had no sooner landed when a British sentry sounded an alarm. Spread out along the riverbank, with the British on Queenstown Heights, the Americans were sitting ducks, and nine officers and 45 enlisted men were soon dead. However, the Americans managed to struggle to the high ground and began shooting effectively. One bullet struck and killed General Brock. As British troops rushed to avenge his death, Van Rensselaer realized that a possible victory was slipping away. On the opposite side of the river, he tried to get fresh troops to cross, but no

The American invasion at Queenstown failed when reinforcements refused to cross the Niagara River. *(National Archives of Canada/C-23304)*

matter how hard he pleaded, the inexperienced militiamen refused to go: "I found that at the very moment when complete victory was in our hands, the Ardor of the unengaged Troops had entirely subsided. . . . I rode in all directions—urged men by every consideration to pass over, but in vain."

A short time later, the Americans on the other side of the river—exhausted and with their cartridge boxes empty—raised the white flag. Some had tried to swim back but drowned in the swift Niagara River. Those who surrendered would later be exchanged for prisoners, and some—such as Colonel Scott—would go on to distinguish themselves in other battles.

Meanwhile, as part of General Dearborn's four-prong plan to take Canada, an attack was launched across Lake Ontario. On April 25, 1813, a flotilla of ships left Sackett's Harbor in New York. Two days later, some 1,600 men, commanded by Gen. Zebulon Pike (a noted explorer after

The garrison at York, the military base for Upper Canada, was the initial target of invading American forces. After an explosion killed more than

whom Pikes Peak in Colorado is named), landed at York (present-day Toronto), the capital of Upper Canada. Under cover of naval bombardment, the American troops attacked the 800 British and Indian soldiers defending York. With superior forces and naval support, it did not take long for Pike's army to overwhelm the enemy, killing 60, wounding 89, and capturing 290.

Unfortunately, American casualties were even higher, due to a terrifying explosion in the garrison's ammunition storeroom. The blast from

300 of their number, however, Americans sacked the entire city in revenge. *(Sempronius Stretton/National Archives of Canada/G14905)*

hundreds of barrels of gunpowder and a huge amount of ammunition caused more than 300 deaths, including that of Pike himself, who was killed by a large falling stone that crushed his chest. American army surgeons worked round the clock, wading in blood and "cutting off arms, legs and trepanning [boring holes] in heads."

Historians disagree as to the cause of the explosion and who was responsible. American soldiers and sailors, however, were furious at the loss of life and determined on revenge. Over the next four days they not only destroyed two unfinished British frigates and all the military and naval supplies in York. They also torched the city's parliamentary and other public buildings, demolished a printing press, and sacked "every house they found deserted." The British would later use this episode as a reason for burning Washington, D.C.

In the months after the attack on York, there were other battles in the northwestern sector. Gen. William Henry Harrison had been gathering his forces at Fort Meigs, on the Maumee River in Ohio. In May 1813, British forces led by General Proctor, supported by Tecumseh and some of his warriors, attacked the fort, but they were held off for eight days before they abandoned the attempt. However, the British and Indians did surprise a unit of Kentuckians who were making their way to reinforce Harrison's forces at Fort Meigs. Hundreds of Americans were killed or captured, and some of the Indians began to massacre even the prisoners. Tecumseh came riding up on horseback and intervened to stop the slaughter, actually striking his own warriors with the flat side of his tomahawk. Then, it is said, Tecumseh rode up to Proctor and scolded him severely, saying: "Begone! You are unfit to command. I conquer to save, and you to murder."

In late July Proctor returned to lay siege to Fort Meigs, but again Harrison's men repulsed the British and Indians. Proctor then moved on to attack Fort Stephenson, also in Ohio some 25 miles east of Fort Meigs. Since Maj. George Croghan had only 160 men in the fort and Proctor had some 1,400, Harrison ordered Croghan to abandon the fort. Croghan, only 23 years old, sent back the reply: "We have determined to maintain this place, and by heaven, we will." The Kentucky riflemen in the fort were sharpshooters and held off repeated charges by the British troops. After a while Proctor called off the attack and went back to Fort Malden.

By September 1813, there was a turnaround in the situation along the U.S.-Canadian border, although it had little to do with Dearborn's four-pronged strategy and more to do with the victory of Oliver Hazard Perry on Lake Erie. With Lake Erie now controlled by the Americans, the British were no longer able to move supplies so easily from the east to the west. Accordingly, Proctor decided to abandon Fort Malden and retreat northeastward up the Thames River, a move that would stretch the Americans' own supply lines.

Tecumseh bitterly opposed Proctor's decision. Why were the British leaving after only one defeat? If they left, it would mean the end of the

Indians' struggle to keep their ancestral hunting grounds. Tecumseh's words, recorded by the British, turned out to be prophetic:

> You always told us to remain here and take care of our land. . . . You always told us you would never draw your foot off British ground; but now, father, we see that you are drawing back, and we are sorry to see our father doing so without seeing the enemy. We must compare our father's conduct to a fat dog, that carries his tail on his back, but when frightened, drops it between his legs and runs off. . . . Father, you have got the arms and ammunition which our great father [the British king] sent for his children. If you have any idea of going away, give them to us, and you may go and welcome. Our lives arc in the hands of the great Spirit. We are determined to defend our lands, and if it be His will, we wish to leave our bones upon it.

But Proctor felt he had no choice, and Tecumseh reluctantly agreed to accompany the British. Abandoning Fort Malden on September 24, 1813, Proctor proceeded along the north bank of the Thames River, with Harrison and an American army of 9,500 men in hot pursuit. On October 5, the ragged, dispirited enemy—numbering about 600–800 British regulars and 500–1,000 Indians—made a stand about one and one-half miles from Moraviantown.

The battle lasted about one hour. The British line collapsed in less than five minutes. The Indians were harder to defeat. Fighting from the underbrush, they tried to repulse Harrison's troops, pressing them back towards the road. It was reported by Americans that they could hear Tecumseh's cry above the din of battle, "Be brave, be brave!" And then he was heard no more.

There have been many questions concerning the circumstances surrounding Tecumseh's death. Some claimed they saw the Indian chief fall with a gunshot wound in his chest. Others claimed to have seen his body after some Kentuckians—in revenge for the Raisin River massacre—cut strips of skin from its thighs and other areas to make into souvenir pouches. What seems much more likely is that Tecumseh's body was taken away by his warriors under cover of darkness and secretly buried. In any event, what mattered most was that his death marked the end of the dream of confederation among the northern tribes.

Casualties in the Battle of the Thames were surprisingly light. Seven Americans were killed and 22 wounded, compared to 18 British soldiers

The death of Tecumseh at the Battle of the Thames. The exact circumstances of his death remain uncertain. *(Library of Congress)*

killed and 25 wounded. More than 600 British soldiers were taken prisoner, and about $1 million worth of weapons was captured. Only 33 bodies of Indians were found, and historians believe that most of the dead Indians—like Tecumseh—were carried away from the battlefield at night.

The outcome of the battle affected the two commanding generals in different ways. Proctor reached safety but was court-martialed and "suspended from rank and pay" for six months. Harrison did not pursue the enemy further but returned to Washington a conquering hero. The Northwest Territory was once more in American hands.

There would be several more battles along the Canadian frontier in the central and eastern sectors, with each side winning its share and nothing truly decisive resulting. As part of the grand strategy that called for taking Montreal, the American generals Wade Hampton and James Wilkinson led their forces toward that city in the fall of 1813, but each turned back after minor engagements near the St. Lawrence River— at Châteaugay on October 25 for Hampton, at Chrysler's Farm on

November 11 for Wilkinson. In December 1813, the British conquered Fort George and Fort Niagara on Lake Ontario. On July 3, 1814, Gen. Jacob Brown took 5,000 American troops across the Niagara River and captured Fort Erie opposite Buffalo, New York. Two days later, one of General Brown's subordinates, Gen. Winfield Scott, led American troops in a victory over the British in a field at Chippewa, just north of

Financing the War

WHILE THE WAR HAWKS PUSHED FOR WAR WITH Great Britain, they also pushed against the Bank of the United States. Having been elected with the help of state banks, the War Hawks wanted them, rather than the Bank of the United States, to serve as depositories for federal funds. That would enable the state banks to issue more banknotes and increase their business. The difficulty was that the Bank of the United States was the only way the federal government could borrow money.

In 1811, Congress defeated a motion to recharter the Bank of the United States. It then raised soldiers' pay and offered bonuses for enlistments, but adjourned without increasing taxes to cover the new expenditures.

The result was that on March 5, 1813, Secretary of the Treasury Albert Gallatin informed President Madison that the federal government would be flat broke by the end of the month. Congress then authorized Gallatin to borrow $16 million. But he was able to raise less than $6 million.

At this point, the richest man in the United States came to the rescue. Stephen Girard of Philadelphia owned a large fleet of merchant ships, as well as a bank. Several businessmen had promised Gallatin an additional $2 million provided Girard assumed the remaining $8 million. Girard agreed. He asked only that the Treasury keep the loan's proceeds in his bank and pay him a commission of .25 percent on whatever part of the loan he was able to sell to the public. Americans apparently had more confidence in Girard than in the federal government, for within 10 days he sold more than $4.5 million in banknotes. He and some friends assumed the remainder of the loan. The United States was now able to pay for the War of 1812.

Fort Erie. And on July 25, troops under General Brown and General Scott engaged the British at Lundy's Lane, just north of Chippewa, in one of the most fiercely contested battles of the war. Both generals were wounded and both sides suffered extremely heavy casualties. Although the battle ended in a standoff, it diminished the British threat in this central sector of the Canadian front.

But the British in Canada now held the advantage in terms of experienced troops. To the east, Prevost had 10,000 British regulars gathered outside Montreal. In September 1814, he set off to invade the United States, and by September 6 he reached Plattsburg, New York, at the western tip of Lake Champlain. The Americans could count on only some 1,500 regulars and a few thousand militia. In the end, though, the Battle of Plattsburg was to be fought on the water. And although that particular battle was a clear American victory, it meant only that the British were turned back from their own invasion plan. It did not enable the

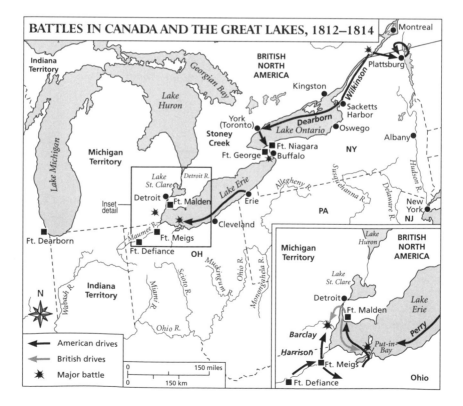

BATTLES IN CANADA AND THE GREAT LAKES, 1812–1814

The Battle of Chippewa and other American incursions into Canada resulted in U.S. victories but did not deliver control of Canada to the United States as hoped. *(National Archives, Still Pictures Branch, NWDNS-111-SC-96967)*

Americans to take any part of Canada. All the many battles fought from the Michigan peninsula to Montreal, from the Raisin River to Lake Champlain, all the thousands of casualties on both sides, all had resulted in a stalemate. The grand goal of capturing Canada would come to nothing.

6

THE NAVAL WAR

While the American forces on the ground were taking heavy casualties and failing to achieve the goal of capturing Canada, another war—the naval war—was being fought on the world's oceans and North America's lakes. There, too, the balance of victories and defeats shifted between the two nations. Considering how mismatched the British and American navies were, it can be regarded as an extraordinary achievement that the Americans did as well as they did.

In 1812 Britannia did indeed rule the waves. The Royal Navy was larger than the combined navies of any two other nations in the world. It contained 1,048 warships, about half of them battleships and frigates. The British ships carried some 28,000 cannons and were manned by approximately 158,000 seamen. In contrast, the U.S. Navy consisted of 16 warships, 442 guns, and 5,000 men. British naval officers referred sneeringly to the American ships as "bundles of pine boards" with "bits of striped rag floating over them." In addition to being about 65 times the size of the American navy, the Royal Navy had an enviable record of victories. Over the past 14 years of warfare with France, it had lost only two of 400 encounters at sea.

That said, the U.S. Navy did have to its credit the exploits of the Barbary War, which had given some young officers valuable experience. Furthermore, Great Britain was still heavily engaged in its war with France, and the Royal Navy chose to assign only a few ships to the American sphere. Also, many of the British sailors had been forced into service and were disciplined by the harshest of measures—short rations, brutal floggings, and executions for all kinds of

Building the USS Constitution

IN 1794 CONGRESS APPROVED CONSTRUCTION OF THREE war frigates for the U.S. Navy. The last to be finished was the *Constitution,* which was launched in July 1797 in Boston Harbor.

The *Constitution* was one of the largest warships then in existence. Designed by Joshua Humphreys, it measured about 200 feet by 50 feet and weighed more than 2,000 tons. Approximately 1,500 trees were cut down to make the lumber needed. The deck and hull planking were made of white oak, which is both strong and durable. The deck beams were made of pitch pine. White pine trees 200 feet tall were turned into masts and spars.

The hull of the *Constitution* boasted two innovations. On most ships of that period, the frames, or ribs, were spaced at least two feet apart. Humphreys left only two inches between the *Constitution's* frames. He filled in the intervening space with crushed rock salt to help preserve the wood. Planks were then attached to both sides of the frames with pegs made of locust wood. This created what was in effect a solid wood wall almost two feet thick that was able to repel cannonballs. (No wonder the *Constitution* was later nicknamed "Old Ironsides.") Humphrey's second innovation was the use of copper sheathing on the part of the hull below the waterline. Copper kept off the barnacles that reduced a ship's speed. The *Constitution's* sheathing, which came from England, was crafted by famed silversmith Paul Revere. The *Constitution* carried 40 sails on its three masts, more sail than other frigates. The main topsail was 80 feet wide and 50 feet high and weighed as much as half a ton. Raising and lowering it required a lot of hard work.

offenses. Morale among the lower ranks was poor compared to that of American sailors, who were fighting to protect their own land and loved ones.

Moreover, although the U.S. Navy was minuscule compared to the Royal Navy, its ships were well built and its sailors well trained. Only the best materials went into American ships: thick boards of oak, cedar, and pine; tall, straight masts of fir; spikes and anchors carefully crafted out of iron; and copper bolts and sheeting to protect the ships' bottoms and keep sea worms from boring into the wood. American naval gunners practiced rapid loading and target shooting at every opportunity. In contrast, British crews practiced their gunnery only once or twice a year.

Still, most Americans considered it foolhardy, if not impossible, for the U.S. Navy to fight the Royal Navy. Instead, American ship captains were told to concentrate on interfering with British commerce. As matters turned out, however, the U.S. Navy *did* engage in several battles with British warships and succeeded in winning a number of the encounters.

By a quirk of fate, the man who delivered the first American victory at sea was Capt. Isaac Hull, nephew of the disgraced Gen. William Hull. Isaac Hull had gone to sea at the age of 14 and had served in the war against Tripoli. When the War of 1812 broke out, he was in command of the frigate *Constitution*. He was ordered to finish assembling a crew of 450 sailors and marines—of whom about one in six was a free black— at Annapolis and then proceed northward along the coast. On July 5, 1812, the *Constitution* set sail.

On July 16, a lookout spotted some ships on the horizon. By five o'clock the next morning, they turned out to be a British fleet of four frigates and one ship of the line, or battleship. Against odds of five to one, Hull decided to make a run for it. But there was little or no wind, and it was difficult to move the *Constitution*. First Hull ordered rowboats lowered to tow the ship. Then he tried kedging, which consisted of dropping a 4,700-pound kedge, or anchor, ahead of the *Constitution*, pulling the anchor cable in until the ship was abreast of the kedge, and then repeating the process. When a breeze came up, Hull ordered the crew to water down the sails, since a wet sail will hold more wind than a dry one. Each time Hull tried a new maneuver, the British did the same.

For two days the chase continued, while Hull remained at his command post on deck, not even taking time off to sleep. At last the *Constitution* eluded the enemy and on July 26 entered Boston Harbor. As a later captain of the ship said, Hull's exploit was "a 57-hour demonstration of endurance, teamwork, and skilled seamanship." Within the month, Hull would offer Americans even more exciting news.

In early August, the *Constitution* put out to sea in search of enemy cargo ships attempting to bring supplies to Canada. On August 19, Hull came upon the British warship *Guerrière*. Both ships immediately prepared for action. Drummer boys beat out the call to battle stations. Gunners opened the gun ports, rammed powder charges down the cannon barrels, and stood ready to fire. Marine snipers with muskets

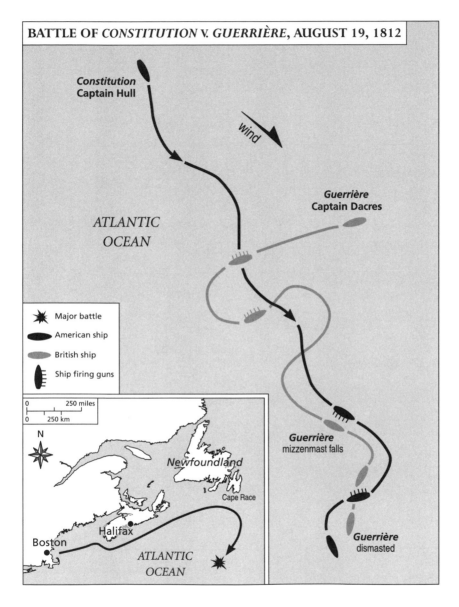

BATTLE OF *CONSTITUTION* V. *GUERRIÈRE*, AUGUST 19, 1812

Constitution
Captain Hull

wind

Guerrière
Captain Dacres

ATLANTIC
OCEAN

Major battle

American ship

British ship

Ship firing guns

0   250 miles
0   250 km

N

Newfoundland

Cape Race

Halifax

Boston

ATLANTIC
OCEAN

Guerrière
mizzenmast falls

Guerrière
dismasted

climbed the rigging and stationed themselves in the crow's-nests on top
of the masts. Below deck, the ships' surgeons cleared areas for tables and
the equipment they would use to operate: saws, knives, scissors, needles,
and thread.

Capt. James Dacres of the 38-gun *Guerrière* fired first, but most of his shots either fell short or were aimed too high. Hull held his fire until his ship was within 50 yards of the enemy. Then the *Constitution's* 54 guns thundered at the *Guerrière,* forcing it to "reel and tremble as though she had received the shock of an earthquake." There was little the enemy could do in response. Even the few British cannonballs that struck the *Constitution* bounced off her heavily timbered hull. "Huzza! Her sides are made of iron!" an American sailor is said to have shouted, thus giving the *Constitution* her famous nickname, "Old Ironsides."

After two and one-half hours, Dacres had no alternative but to surrender the *Guerrière.* As Hull reported, "She was left without a Spar Standing, and the Hull cut to pieces, in such a manner as to make it difficult to keep her above water." British casualties totaled 23 dead and 56 wounded. The Americans suffered seven dead and seven wounded.

Too shattered to be of any use, the *Guerrière* was set afire. Moses Smith, a sailor on the *Constitution,* described the scene as follows:

> We set a slow match to her magazine and left her. At a distance of about three miles we hove to. . . . The grand crash came. The quarter deck, immediately above the magazine, lifted in a mass and flew in every direction. The hull parted, and sank out of sight. It was a grand and awful scene. We immediately squared away under a cloud of sail for our native land.

When the *Constitution* came into Boston Harbor, the city went wild. On the ship's mast, below the Stars and Stripes, fluttered a British battleflag. The Royal Navy was not invincible after all.

Within the next several months, American warships would score several more resounding victories against the British: the U.S. sloop-of-war *Wasp* defeated HMS *Frolic;* the USS *Hornet* sank HMS *Peacock;* the USS *Constitution,* this time commanded by Capt. William Bainbridge, destroyed HMS *Java.* The most celebrated of these battles occurred on October 25, 1812. The *United States,* commanded by Stephen Decatur of Barbary War fame, came upon the British frigate *Macedonian* some 600 miles off the west coast of Africa. Decatur's gunners succeeded in firing 70 broadsides to the British 30. The American bombardment destroyed most of the *Macedonian's* masts and rigging and killed or wounded 74 men, about one-third of its crew. American casualties numbered 12 (five dead, seven wounded). Decatur then put a prize crew

The battle of the USS *Constitution* and the *Guerrière* was a resounding victory for the new U.S. Navy. *(Library of Congress)*

aboard the *Macedonian* to sail the ship to New England. It was the first time that a British frigate had been brought into an American port, and the event lifted American pride. As one Republican crowed, "British arms cannot withstand American upon the sea. The bully has been disgraced by an infant."

American privateers were also bringing in prizes. A privateer was a privately owned vessel commissioned by the government to fight against enemy shipping. Being commissioned meant that if the ship's crew were captured, they would be treated as prisoners of war instead of being hung for piracy. Serving on a privateer was more attractive to many sailors than serving in the U.S. Navy. A privateer offered the opportunity of profits, less chance of being involved in a naval battle, and two or three months' service as compared with the navy's expectation of one year of duty. In the first six months of the War of 1812, American privateers—known as Baltimore clippers ("clipper" being a slang word for "fast")—captured 450 British merchant vessels on the high seas. One Republican called the privateers "our cheapest and best Navy." In response, the U.S. Navy began offering incentives, such as bonuses, to bring more sailors on board. Thus, the officers and crew of the *United States* shared $200,000 in prize money for capturing the *Macedonian.*

The American successes at sea shocked and dismayed the British. The London *Times* asked plaintively, "What is wrong with British sea power?" and asserted that "There is one object to which our most strenuous efforts should be directed—the entire annihilation of the American Navy." Accordingly, the Royal Navy blockaded the eastern shores of the United States. However, with the exception of Boston Harbor, the blockade never extended to New England, probably because American merchants there were carrying on a treasonous trade in foodstuffs with both Canada and Great Britain.

By the winter of 1813, the blockade had succeeded in bottling up most of the U.S. Navy. Only three American frigates remained at sea: the *President,* the *Congress,* and the *Essex.* However, until it was captured on March 22, 1814, the *Essex* succeeded in doing considerable damage to British commerce.

The commander of the *Essex* was Capt. David Porter, "a sour-faced Bostonian with a grudge against the Royal Navy." Impressed aboard a British ship when he was 17 years old, Porter had jumped overboard and swum through shark-infested waters to safety. The following year, he was impressed again, and again he escaped. Porter was a strict captain. He would issue fire alarms and boarding alarms at night to make certain that his crew was always alert. Sailors who were slow to respond were put on a diet of bread and water for one week, while repeated offenders were tossed in the ship's brig.

On October 28, 1812, Porter left Delaware Bay and headed into the South Atlantic. On February 14, 1813, he rounded Cape Horn and entered the Pacific Ocean. His target was the British whaling fleet, which each year sent back to England millions of dollars worth of whale oil to be burned in lamps.

Because the *Essex* was the first American warship to enter the Pacific, the British whalers there were taken by surprise. They were not even protected by the Royal Navy! Between April and September, Porter captured 12 whalers, 360 British seamen, and whale oil worth about $2.5 million. He also lived off the enemy, removing food, medicines, rope, tar, and other supplies from each whaler as he captured it. Porter burned most of his prizes. However, he put his prisoners aboard one of the whalers and set them free. He also converted another whaler into a mini-warship that he named *Essex Jr.*

THE NAVAL WAR

In March 1814, Porter made a stopover at Valparaíso, Chile. But by this time the Royal Navy had been alerted to the *Essex*'s exploits. No sooner had Porter entered the neutral port than he found the harbor blocked by two British warships, the frigate *Phoebe* and the sloop *Cherub*. Realizing that the enemy had six guns to his one, Porter tried to escape. But a sudden strong wind swept away the *Essex*'s main masts and sails, leaving the ship unable to maneuver. For two hours, the *Phoebe* and the *Cherub* poured one murderous round after another into the helpless *Essex*. Finally, realizing that further resistance was hopeless, Porter surrendered. He had lost 58 men killed, 66 wounded, and 31 missing. The British loss was five killed and 10 wounded.

The surrender of the *Essex* and the *Essex Jr.* more or less marked the end of the U.S. Navy's exploits on the high seas. In the meantime, however, another struggle between British and American ships and sailors had shaped up. It started in the spring of 1813 on the Great Lakes.

By that time, it was obvious that American forces would not be able to wrest Canada from British hands unless the United States controlled the Great Lakes, particularly Lake Erie and Lake Ontario. The inland seas

Commanded by Capt. David Porter, the U.S. frigate *Essex* preyed on British whaling ships in the Pacific to disrupt the lucrative traffic in whale oil. *(National Archives, Still Pictures Branch, NWDNS-19-N-13279.)*

Combat at Sea

NAVAL ENGAGEMENTS BETWEEN TWO SHIPS USUALLY began with a chase, during which both ships shot at each other with the guns that were mounted in their bow and stern. As soon as one captain had the wind at his back, he approached to within 50 yards of the enemy. The two ships then traded broadsides with their side-mounted cannons, which were far more numerous than their bow-and-stern guns.

The cannons fired three kinds of shot: (1) solid shot, or iron balls weighing between 12 and 32 pounds each that could damage a ship's hull; (2) chain shot, or two balls joined by a chain that cut anything in their path as they whirled through the air; and (3) grapeshot, or small iron balls that were particularly dangerous to sailors as they exploded from a larger ball.

Sometimes the crew of one ship would try to board the other ship and engage in hand-to-hand combat with cutlasses, knives, and pistols. Boarding, however, was a difficult maneuver that required both skill and luck. It was much more common for the faster ship to pull ahead of its opponent and then turn sideways. That enabled it to rake the enemy's decks with gunfire from its side-mounted cannons. This usually caused so much damage that the slower ship surrendered at once.

were the most efficient means of transporting men and supplies in a heavily wooded, almost roadless region.

President Madison now made an important move when he replaced Secretary of the Navy Paul Hamilton—a gentleman rarely sober enough to conduct business in the afternoon—with William Jones, a Philadelphia merchant mariner. Madison then chose Capt. Isaac Chauncey, a somewhat pompous 40-year-old navy veteran, to command American naval forces on Lakes Erie and Ontario. One of his first actions—in April 1813—was to call for the combined naval and army force that attacked York, capital of Upper Canada. Although it may have provided passing satisfaction to Americans to destroy York, of more far-reaching significance was the fleet that Secretary Jones and Captain Chauncey now commenced to construct on Lake Erie. It was decided to use Presque Isle (now Erie, Pennsylvania) as the construction site. Then the question arose of who should supervise the construction, train the crews, and lead the flotilla against the British.

Chauncey found the answer in the person of 28-year-old Oliver Hazard Perry, then only a master commandant, a rank not nearly as important as it sounds. Perry came from a Quaker family of seamen. His father was a retired naval captain, and his brother, Matthew, would later gain

Oliver Hazard Perry was a brilliant commander of the U.S. naval forces. *(Library of Congress)*

fame for opening Japan to the West (1854). Oliver Perry was a quiet, courteous man who, unlike most naval officers, never used profanity. He was well-read, a superb horseman, and an accomplished flutist. He was also a very moral person. In those days, it was customary for a commander to get a percentage of the construction costs when new ships were being built. Chauncey, for example, was amassing a small fortune at Sackett's Harbor. Perry, however, refused to take a penny. As he explained, "It might influence my judgement and cause people to question my good faith."

Perry's biggest problem turned out to be a shortage of able seamen. Chauncey had given him free rein on Lake Erie but, according to Perry, had kept the best sailors for himself. So Perry scoured the countryside, offering a bonus of $10 for four months' service to every farmer, woodsman, and mechanic in the area. Finally, Gen. William Henry Harrison came to Perry's rescue. Harrison sent all the seamen and marines he could find in his army and added 100 of his best Kentucky sharpshooters, men who could "shoot the whiskers off a squirrel."

By September 1813, the Lake Erie fleet of 11 vessels was ready for action. Perry named his flagship the *Lawrence*, after Capt. James Lawrence of the *Chesapeake*, the frigate that had been defeated by the *Leopard* in 1807. Several months earlier, on June 1, 1813, the *Chesapeake* had been captured by the British outside Boston Harbor and Lawrence had been mortally wounded. As he lay dying, his whispered last words to his men were, "Don't give up the ship." Those words became the motto and rallying cry of America's young navy, and Perry had them sewn in white letters a foot high on the nine-foot-square blue flag that fluttered above his flagship. Commanding the *Lawrence*'s sister ship, the *Niagara*, was Lt. James Elliott.

Perry's counterpart was Capt. Robert Barclay, an experienced commander who had lost an arm in battle. Like Perry, Barclay was short of competent seamen. He was also racing to finish the *Detroit*, a ship about 15 feet longer than the *Lawrence*. However, he lacked the necessary armament for the *Detroit* because much of it had been destroyed or captured at the Battle of York. He was also desperately in need of provisions, since much of the local food supply was being used to feed 14,000 Indians at Amherstburg. "So perfectly destitute of provisions was the port," wrote Barclay, "that there was not a day's flour in store, and the crews of the squadron under my command were on half allowances of many things, and when that was done there was no more."

THE NAVAL WAR

On September 10, at 7:00 A.M., Perry and Barclay faced off. The *Lawrence* was in the lead, accompanied by two gunboats. Elliott was supposed to come up shortly with the *Niagara* and the rest of the American fleet. Perry's strength lay in his short-range smashers. Barclay relied on his long-range guns.

At 11:45 A.M. Barclay opened fire. Round after round tore through the *Lawrence*'s bulwarks, and the ship's deck was soon awash in blood, tangled rigging, and dying men. Where was Elliott with the rest of the American fleet? The question was later raised not only by historians but by Perry as well. Was Elliott hewing to Perry's command and keeping his place in line? Was he angry because a younger man had been given command? Or was he holding back so that he could come forward at the end and save the day?

Despite the terrible loss of men, Perry continued on course until the *Lawrence* was in close enough range to hit back effectively. The *Lawrence*'s

Capt. James Lawrence, fatally wounded while commanding the USS *Chesapeake*, urged his men: "Don't give up the ship!" His words became a rallying cry for American sailors. *(Library of Congress) (National Archives, Still Pictures Branch, NWDNS-111-SC-96966)*

Before its capture, the Canadian flagship *Detroit* inflicted so much damage to the U.S. flagship that Oliver Perry transferred command to another U.S. ship in the midst of the Battle of Lake Erie. *(Metropolitan Toronto Reference Library, J. Ross Robertson Collection, T15242)*

guns traded broadside after broadside with the *Detroit* and her sister ship, the *Queen Charlotte*. Perry was everywhere, giving orders, offering a helping hand, propping up a wounded man. Several musket balls passed through his hat but he ignored them.

The fighting went on for two hours. By then the *Lawrence* was foundering. Its guns fell silent, and Barclay believed that Perry was about to surrender. But Perry had spotted the *Niagara* finally coming up fast, and he decided to do something rarely attempted in the midst of battle: transfer command to another flagship. He turned over the *Lawrence* to his first lieutenant and, carrying the flag with the words "Don't give up the ship," got into a small rowboat with four other men. Fifteen minutes later, having dodged a hail of gunfire, he was aboard the *Niagara* and had taken charge.

Perry ordered the *Niagara* to head directly through the center of the British line of ships. As they closed in, the Americans blasted away with every cannon and musket on board. Inspired by Perry's action, the remaining American ships followed their leader. In short order, every British commander and second-in-command was hit, including Barclay. The *Detroit's* masts crumbled. Two of the remaining British ships caught on fire.

Eight minutes after Perry broke the British line, the *Detroit* ran up the white flag. The other British ships followed suit, and by 3:00 P.M. it was all over. Perry had snatched victory from what had seemed a certain defeat. It was the first time that an entire British fleet had been captured. But the casualties were high: 27 American dead and 96 wounded, 41 British dead and 94 wounded.

Finding a quiet spot on the *Niagara's* deck and using a hat as his desk, Perry scribbled a message to General Harrison in pencil on the back of an old envelope. "We have met the enemy and they are ours."

Perry's victory signaled a turnaround in the situation along the U.S.-Canada border. With Lake Erie now controlled by the Americans, the British were no longer able to get supplies. In addition, the naval defeat had seriously weakened Tecumseh's hold over the Indians, many of whom slowly began to slip away.

It would be almost exactly one year after the defeat of the British fleet on Lake Erie that the final and decisive naval battle between the two nations would take place. It would occur on a North American lake—Lake Champlain. But unlike the battle on Lake Erie, this one was not anticipated by either side to be crucial. Rather, Lake Champlain was regarded by the British as merely a way station that they intended to exploit as they moved their land forces south from Canada to conquer New York State.

Ever since the defeat of Napoleon in April 1814 had freed up British forces in Europe, the British had been assembling a large army at Montreal. Under Lt. Gen. Sir George Prevost, that force by September 1814 stood at about 15,000 men. In contrast, the American ground forces at

Plattsburg—the main settlement at the northwest corner of Lake Champlain—at first numbered only about 3,400, about half of whom were too sick or untrained to be of much use. Fortunately, the fact that Vermont faced invasion of its home territory led some 2,500 Vermont militiamen to volunteer to fight outside their state's borders. An additional 800 militiamen from New York State now also joined up. Still, that left American soldiers outnumbered about three to one.

The situation with regard to the opposing fleets on Lake Champlain, however, was more nearly equal. The British naval forces there consisted of 19 vessels, the American of 16. The British ships carried more guns, but the American batteries were able to fire faster. Each fleet was manned by about 800 soldiers and marines.

Prevost brought his army down to the area of Plattsburg by early September. North of Plattsburg was a series of small forts, and Prevost realized that he should probably first gain control of the northern section of the lake before assaulting these forts and Plattsburg itself.

Capt. Thomas Macdonough, commander of the American flotilla, had taken part in Decatur's attack on Tripoli during the Barbary War.

Oliver Perry during the Battle of Lake Erie *(National Archives, Still Pictures Branch, NWDNS-127-N-302099)*

African-American Sailors

ABOUT ONE-SIXTH OF THE SAILORS WHO SERVED ON U.S. warships and privateers during the War of 1812 were African Americans. Some 100 of them helped Oliver Hazard Perry defeat the British on Lake Erie in September 1813. Perry had complained at first about being sent "only blacks, soldiers, and boys" to man his ships. Capt. Isaac Chauncey, however, felt that Perry should be pleased with his black sailors. "They are not surpassed by any seamen we have in the fleet," Chauncey said, "and I have yet to learn that the color of a man's skin or the cut and trimmings of the coat can affect a man's qualifications or usefulness. I have nearly fifty blacks on board this ship, and many of them are among my best men."

After the battle of Lake Erie, Perry changed his mind about the fighting ability of African Americans. The blacks in his crew, he wrote "seemed absolutely insensible to danger."

There were black sailors in the Royal Navy as well. Some 5,000 slaves from the Chesapeake Bay area ran away from their owners to join the British, who promised them freedom either in Canada or the West Indies. A unit of "Black Marines" under Rear Adm. George Cockburn took part in the fighting at Bladensburg and the burning of Washington, D.C. A popular British song called "The Guinea Boy" told the story of one of these black volunteers.

He had been stationed on Lake Champlain ever since the start of the War of 1812 and so far had not had a chance to fight the enemy. Now he welcomed the opportunity to finally win glory in battle. Knowing that he could not beat the British in open waters where their long guns could destroy his ships, Macdonough stationed his fleet in Plattsburg Bay. He strung his ships like a line of cable across the narrow body of water. Once the British fleet under Capt. George Downie entered the bay, Macdonough's short-range guns would be effective.

On September 11, at 8:00 A.M., Downie's ships came into sight of the American fleet. The battle was quickly joined. It was a grueling, vicious, seesaw struggle, with first one side and then the other firing salvo after salvo at their opponents. Losses on both sides were heavy. American casualties were 22 killed and 58 wounded, while the British lost some 200 men. Downie was killed in a freak accident when an

A song sheet celebrating the American victory at Lake Champlain *(Library of Congress)*

NAVAL BATTLES IN THE ATLANTIC OCEAN, 1812–1813

American cannon shot knocked a British gun from its carriage and sent it smashing into the captain's groin. The blow did not even break the skin, but it killed Downie instantly. Macdonough was knocked unconscious three times in the course of the fighting but revived each time and returned to his command. Finally, after two hours and 20 minutes, Macdonough's skill in maneuvering his ships won the day, and the entire British fleet surrendered. Only the small enemy gunboats managed to row away.

Led by Capt. Macdonough, the American fleet turns back the invading British at the Battle of Plattsburg, New York, one of the hardest-fought contests in the War of 1812. *(National Archives of Canada/C-6240)*

Prevost had waited for news of the naval battle before taking action on land, just assuming the British fleet would prevail. When Prevost's officers learned of its defeat, they offered to attack the American land positions at Plattsburg anyway. Prevost, always a cautious man, was reluctant to do anything without naval support from the lake. Then a local Irishwoman gave Prevost a letter supposedly written by a Vermont colonel to the commander of the American army at Plattsburg, General Macomb. The letter stated that 10,000 volunteers were on their way to aid him. Prevost promptly removed his guns from the batteries and withdrew his troops north to Montreal

The letter turned out to be a fraud. Macomb had played the same trick on Prevost that Britain's general Brock had used to scare America's

general Hull into thinking he was surrounded by Indians at Fort Detroit. True, the trick would probably not have worked had the British fleet not been defeated on Lake Champlain. And when news of the outcome of this Battle of Plattsburg reached England and Europe in mid-October 1814, it would have a major impact on those calling for a negotiated end to the war. But as important as the American victories on Lake Erie and Lake Champlain were, the fact remained that by the autumn of 1814 most of the American navy was in hiding from the powerful British blockade along the Atlantic coast. American privateers, to be sure, were taking a toll of British shipping. But in the end, America's and Britain's naval forces were proving to be no more able to bring the war to a conclusion than were their land forces.

7

"O'ER THE LAND OF THE FREE"

Some six months before the Battle of Plattsburg, in April 1814, Great Britain and its European allies had decisively defeated Napoleon. With France no longer a problem, Britain was free to devote all its energies to concluding its frustrating war with the United States. The subsequent victory of the American fleet on Lake Champlain and the withdrawal of British troops to Montreal represented the effective blunting of one of the three major "prongs" in Great Britain's new, aggressive strategy.

British military leaders had drawn up a three-part plan. One part called for an attack from Canada down Lake Champlain into New York State. The idea was to separate New England from the rest of the United States. Since New Englanders were generally opposed to the war and had been trading with the British throughout the conflict, it was even suggested by some that the New England states might secede and rejoin Great Britain. That part of the plan now seemed to have failed.

A second part of Britain's strategy called for an attack against New Orleans. This would enable the British to cut off trade along the Mississippi and so isolate America's western territories that Britain might even gain control of this land. This part of the plan would soon be put into effect, once sufficient ships and troops had gathered in the Gulf of Mexico.

The third part of Britain's strategy called for a combined army and navy assault to bring "hard war" to prominent American coastal cities: Washington, Baltimore, Charleston, and Savannah. This would serve to

"O'ER THE LAND OF THE FREE"

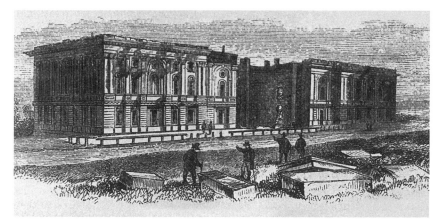

Ruins of the Capitol after the fire *(National Archives, Still Pictures Branch, NWDNS-66-G-21C-31)*

demoralize the American people and might well lead to the collapse of increasingly shaky support for continuing the war.

The humiliating defeat of the Americans at Bladensburg, Maryland, on August 24, 1814, and the ensuing capture and burning of Washington, D.C., on August 24–25, seemed an extremely favorable beginning for the British grand strategy. President Madison and several of his top advisers barely had time to cross the Potomac River ahead of the British. Plans were made to rendezvous at Frederick, Maryland, as soon as possible. Instead, the president and the secretaries of war, state, and navy—anxious to rejoin their families—ended up in four different places. By August 27, however, Madison learned that the British had evacuated Washington. Quickly, the president dispatched messengers instructing his cabinet members to meet him the following day, August 28, in the capital. Madison realized that it was most important to assert the authority of the national government.

The sights that greeted the returning president were appalling. Not only had much of the capital been torched, but looters—poor drifters and unskilled workers—had plundered the burning rubble, snatching at anything they could get their hands on: groceries, clothing, even files in the War Department's vault. Dead bodies lay in doorways, while the wounded in shanties cried out for help. It was estimated that more than 50 people had been killed or injured in the riots that followed the retreat of the American forces.

Quickly, Madison and his cabinet began functioning again. There was talk in Congress and among some citizens about moving the capital to a new and safer location. But Madison stood firm and threatened to veto any such action. The razing of a capital city in Europe would have marked the final blow to national pride and would probably have ended the war. In the United States, it had quite the opposite effect.

The spunky action of the president and his cabinet in reconvening as quickly as they did impressed American citizens. "The President . . .," reported the *National Intelligencer* admiringly, "was not only active during the engagement which took place with the enemy, but had been exerting himself for two or three days previous. . . . Everyone joins in attributing to him the greatest merit." Other newspapers likewise applauded the president's action as despair over the American defeat at Bladensburg and the burning of Washington turned into a determination to take revenge. "The Spirit of the Nation is roused," announced the Baltimore *Register*. ". . . War is a new business to us, but we must 'teach our fingers to fight.'" Antiadministration papers, such as the Albany *Register,* called on Americans to pull together in the crisis. "Let one voice and one spirit animate us all—the voice of our bleeding country and the spirit of our immortal ancestors." Everywhere, even in states that had opposed "Mr. Madison's War," Americans flocked to support the war effort, whether with money, labor, or by volunteering for the armed forces.

There was one cabinet member, however, upon whom the citizens of Washington vented their anger over the burning of their city. That was Secretary of War John Armstrong. The people seemed to forget General Winder's poor leadership and other factors that contributed to the Bladensburg disaster. It was all Armstrong's fault! When he returned to the capital, one false charge after another was levied against him. He was plotting to overthrow the American government. He had carried on treasonous communications with a relative in the British army. "The movements of this fiend should be narrowly watched," warned a Georgetown newspaper. Army officers refused to serve if Armstrong resumed his post. "There, sir, are our swords," said a spokesman for the officers. "We will not employ them if General Armstrong is to command us in his capacity of Secretary of War, but we will obey the orders of any other member of the Cabinet." Enlisted men, not having swords, threw down the shovels with which they had been digging ditches to show that they, too, wanted nothing to do with the hapless secretary.

"O'ER THE LAND OF THE FREE"

Secretary of War
John Armstrong
became the scapegoat
of a nation enraged
over the destruction
of its capital. *(Library
of Congress)*

As tactfully as possible, Madison tried to relieve Armstrong of his cabinet post. The president offered him a temporary relief of duty, but Armstrong refused. Instead, on September 3, after four days of smoldering in Baltimore, he announced his resignation in a long and bitter letter to the Baltimore *Patriot and Evening Advertiser.* The following day he sent a brief two-sentence note to the same effect to Madison. The president then asked Secretary of State James Monroe to assume Armstrong's responsibilities temporarily. Monroe was delighted. It was the first time a cabinet member had undertaken two posts simultaneously.

It took only a few days for the city's banks to reopen. From Monticello, Virginia, came an offer from Thomas Jefferson to replace the books in the Library of Congress. The former president had been amassing his collection for 40 years. Although a few shortsighted members of Congress protested the cost, wiser heads prevailed, and Jefferson received $50,000 for what became the basis of today's superb congressional library.

In the meantime, the British continued with the third part of their three-part strategy. With Washington in ruins, Baltimore was next on their agenda. This was logical, for the city was a large commercial center whose populace had been enthusiastically in favor of a war with Britain.

The fall of Baltimore would go a long way toward demoralizing the United States. Equally important, Baltimore was a major base for privateers—and Britain was smarting heavily over the fact that although Britannia was said to rule the waves, one British merchant vessel after another had fallen prey to America's commerce raiders. In fact, many of the prizes had been taken in British coastal waters. For example, the *Governor Tompkins* had captured 14 ships at the mouth of the English Channel. The *Prince of Neufchatel* had decimated traffic in the Irish Channel. And the *Chasseur* had not only spent three months off the British coast, its captain, Thomas Boyle, had had the audacity to notify Lloyd's of London, Britain's premier insurance company, that his blockade extended to "all the ports, harbors, bays, creeks, rivers, inlets, outlets, islands and seacoast of the United Kingdom."

Unlike Washington, however, Baltimore was well prepared to defend itself. Early in 1814, under the able leadership of Samuel Smith, a U.S. senator and a major general in the Maryland militia, the city had begun a campaign to encourage able-bodied persons to volunteer. The local papers even urged elderly men "who are able to carry a firelock (a gun that requires a match to ignite its powder charge) and willing to render a last service to their country and posterity" to form a company. By the time the British assault came, Smith had between 10,000 and 15,000 troops under his command.

He also had the services of three outstanding naval officers. John Rodgers, David Porter, and Oliver Hazard Perry were in port, unable to sail because of the British blockade of the coast. They and their seamen helped with raising fortifications and manning shore guns. Smith also ordered the sinking of several dozen small vessels in Baltimore's harbor so that the large ships of the British fleet would not be able to enter.

Baltimore lay along the banks of the Patapsco River. In front of the city, a peninsula split the river into two channels. At the tip of this peninsula, guarding the city, stood a masonry and earth fort, Fort McHenry. McHenry and its garrison of 1,000 men were commanded by Maj. George Armistead. The previous year, Armistead had said that he wanted "a flag so large that the British will have no difficulty in seeing it from a distance." The flag that now flew over the fort met his wish. Sewn by a widow named Mary Young Pickergill and her 13-year-old daughter Caroline at a cost of $405.90, the flag measured 42 feet by 30 feet. Its eight red and seven white stripes were each two feet wide, and its 15 white stars were two feet across.

Fort McHenry

THE ORIGINAL FORT MCHENRY WAS BUILT DURING THE American Revolution, in 1776. It was then known as Fort Whetstone because it stood on a peninsula called Whetstone Point. The site was well chosen. It was close enough to Baltimore to provide protection, yet it was far enough away that it did not offer a target near the houses of civilians. In addition, enemy ships would have to pass the fort before they could enter Baltimore harbor.

As matters turned out, Baltimore was not attacked during the Revolutionary War, so Fort Whetstone's cannons did not see any action. In 1798, it was decided to build a new fort on Whetstone Point. Designed by a French engineer named Jean Foncin, the new fort was named Fort McHenry after James McHenry, George Washington's secretary of war, who had campaigned energetically for its construction.

The British attack on Fort McHenry during the War of 1812 lasted for some 25 hours, during which time American cannons sank at least 20 British ships. It was the only time in the fort's history that its cannons were fired.

During the Civil War, Union troops were stationed at Fort McHenry to prevent Confederate sympathizers from seizing Baltimore. The fort also served to hold Confederate prisoners of war.

Fort McHenry remained in military service until 1912. From 1915 to 1917, it was used as a city park and beach. In 1917, some 100 temporary buildings were erected on the site to care for returning wounded veterans of World War I. The hospital buildings were torn down in 1925 when Fort McHenry became a national monument. In 1939, it was named the United States's only historic shrine—Fort McHenry National Monument and Historic Shrine.

The British plan of operation was to be a joint land and sea effort. As was the case in the attack on Washington, Gen. Robert Ross was in charge of the troops, while Rear Adm. George Cockburn was in charge of the naval forces.

Before dawn on September 12, 1814, Ross landed some 9,000 men at North Point and began the 14-mile march west to Baltimore. Hoping to delay the enemy, Smith sent out Brig. Gen. John Stricker with five regiments of militia and six guns. Stricker disposed his men at a spot where

George Cockburn commanded the naval forces in England's two-pronged attack on Baltimore.
(Library of Congress)

the only two roads to Baltimore converged into one—and waited. The troops grew impatient as the hours ticked away. Finally, an advance scout brought the news that at 11:00 A.M. the British had halted at the Gorsuch farm and were "feasting and frying." At 1:00 P.M. Stricker decided to provoke a fight and sent an advance party of 250 men toward North Point. A half-mile up the road, they met the enemy. After a sharp skirmish, the Americans fell back to rejoin the main force. But it was hardly a victory for the British, for in the heat of battle Ross galloped to the front on his white horse and was mortally wounded by an American sharpshooter.

The British hit General Stricker's main body of troops at 2:50 P.M. The engagement lasted less than an hour and, as at Bladensburg, the screaming Congreve rockets unnerved the Americans and they were forced to retreat. However, this time they retreated in good order and

regrouped in front of Baltimore. Although their losses were heavy—
33 dead and 115 wounded—British casualties were about twice that
number. Instead of pursuing the Americans, the British—now led by
Col. Arthur Brooke—decided to camp for the night and wait until morning to resume their march toward Baltimore.

Early on the morning of September 13, British naval forces swung into
action and began bombarding Fort McHenry from five bomb and rocket
vessels. Hour after hour, the enemy pounded the fort. But although British
gunners fired between 1,800 and 2,000 cannonballs, damage was minimal.
Only four Americans were killed and 24 wounded. Hour after hour, all
through the day and on into the night, the "rockets' red glare" from the
British ships lit up the sky. As the *Weekly Register* reported, "The attack was
terribly grand and magnificent." But on the morning of September 14,
realizing that they could not breach Baltimore's defenses, "the enemy precipitately retired. Never was the mortification of an invader more complete." Admiral Cockburn withdrew the fleet; Colonel Brooke withdrew
the army. It was a triumph for the United States.

The death of Gen. Robert Ross, commander of British land forces at
Baltimore *(Library of Congress)*

One of those who witnessed "the bombs bursting in air" over Fort McHenry was a 35-year-old lawyer from Georgetown, Maryland, named Francis Scott Key. He had been serving with a volunteer artillery battery at Baltimore but was now on a mission of mercy for President Madison. His task was to repatriate a Dr. William Beanes.

During the British advance on Washington back in August, Dr. Beanes's farm in Upper Marlboro, Maryland, had been used as headquarters by General Ross. A group of stragglers from Ross's army had looted nearby farms, gone on drunken sprees, and terrorized local women. To stop the pillaging, Dr. Beanes and several of his neighbors formed a vigilante group and caught six of the British stragglers. However, a seventh redcoat escaped and reported the capture of his fellow soldiers to a troop of British cavalry. The redcoats thereupon broke into Beanes' home at 1 A.M. and dragged the doctor, wearing only a pair of pants and a nightshirt, before General Ross. Because Beanes had been born in Scotland, he was considered a British subject. That made his action treason, punishable by death. Ross insisted that the doctor be sent to Halifax or Bermuda to stand trial.

When Ross and Cockburn ignored a petition for clemency from the local residents, Francis Scott Key decided to intercede for Beanes with President Madison. The president agreed to Key's proposal and suggested that he get in touch with John S. Skinner, another attorney, who was experienced in negotiating prisoner exchanges. The two men took a small boat flying a white flag of truce and on September 7 caught up with the British fleet at the mouth of the Patapsco River. They boarded the flagship and were cordially invited to stay for dinner.

After dinner, Key and Skinner presented their case to General Ross. Fortunately, Key carried on his person a packet of letters written by British soldiers who were being treated in an American hospital. After reading the letters, which praised the care the soldiers were receiving from American doctors, Ross agreed to release Beanes. But not just yet. As Admiral Cockburn pointed out, "After discussing so freely our preparations and plans [for attacking Baltimore], you could hardly expect us to let you go on shore in advance of us." So for one week Beanes, Key, and Skinner remained on board a British ship.

During the bombardment of Fort McHenry, Key paced the ship's deck all night. In the darkness, it was hard to tell who was winning the battle. But in "the dawn's early light," he was able to see the Stars and Stripes still waving over the fort. The sight inspired Key to jot down some verses on the back of a letter he was carrying. The tune that kept running through his head as he composed the words was an old British drinking song, "To Anacreon in Heaven."

A few days later, Key's verses were published in the *American and Commercial Daily Advertiser* of Baltimore. The song was soon picked up

Francis Scott Key, a young lawyer, wrote "The Star Spangled Banner" while watching the Battle of Fort McHenry from a ship anchored nearby. *(Library of Congress)*

War Songs

THE WORDS TO "THE STAR-SPANGLED BANNER," originally known as "The Defense of Fort McHenry," were set to an old English drinking song within a few days after Francis Scott Key circulated his poem. It became the most famous song to come out of the War of 1812. However, other songs based on the war were also popular. One of them was published in Boston after the *Constitution*'s defeat of the *Guerrière* in 1812. It was set to the tune of another English drinking song. The first verse goes as follows:

It oft-times has been told, that the British seamen bold
Could flog the tars of France so neat and handy, O:
But they never met their match till the Yankees did them catch,
O the Yankee boys for fighting are the dandy, O!

Another song, "The Hunters of Kentucky," was written shortly after the Battle of New Orleans in 1815. The Americans won the battle under the generalship of Andrew Jackson. "The Hunters of Kentucky" later became one of Jackson's campaign songs when he ran for the presidency in 1828. Below is one of the song's verses:

But Jackson he was wide awake, and wasn't scared at trifles,
For well he knew what aim we'd take with our Kentucky rifles:
So he led us down to Cypress swamp, the ground was low and
    mucky,
There stood John Bull in martial pomp, and here was Old
    Kentucky.

The name "John Bull" refers to the British troops. John Bull is the symbol of England, just as Uncle Sam is the symbol of the United States.

by the tavern crowds, with whom it became a great hit. Within a month, it appeared in newspapers throughout the country, from New Hampshire to Georgia. In 1931 the song would be formally adopted as the national anthem of the United States.

But all that lay in the future. The immediate result of the Chesapeake campaign was that the British got back in their ships and left the area.

They had brought "hard war" to two major cities but had only strengthened the resolve of many Americans. Like another prong in their three-part strategy—the Lake Champlain campaign—it had failed in its ultimate goal. Only one prong remained—the seizure of New Orleans. But what had seemed so clear and neat to the British strategists in London was going to run afoul in the tangled situation in the American South.

8

THE WAR
IN THE SOUTH

With the withdrawal of the British from the Chesapeake region and the defeat of their fleet on Lake Champlain—both events occurring in September 1814—the war seemed to have reached another stalemate. The British and Americans had been fighting each other for more than two years by this time, but except in the Washington-Baltimore area and along the Canadian border—and wherever their ships met at sea—the war was having little direct impact on most residents of North America.

There was another exception, however, and that was in parts of the American South. There the war with the British became intertwined with another conflict that Americans were involved in. This other conflict, although apparently separate from the war between the Americans and the British, was in fact directly related to it. This conflict pitted white Americans against the Creek Indians, and the common links between it and the War of 1812 were forged by two notable individuals, Tecumseh and Andrew Jackson.

The Creek inhabited what is now central Georgia, northern Florida, and Alabama. They actually called themselves the Muskogee, after the language they spoke. They were known to white Americans as the Creek because the English had originally applied that name to a group of Muskogee who lived near a creek.

Like other Native Americans, the Creek regarded the fields and streams of their homeland as part of their culture and religion, never to be divided. By contrast, the white European colonists looked at "unsettled" land as lying fallow, waiting to be cleared for farms, roads, and towns. And as more and more whites settled on what had been Muskogee territory, the United States demanded the cession of more and more land by the Creek. Yet the new boundaries never seemed to satisfy the pioneers, who continued to encroach on Indian land and kill off herds of deer and other animals on the Creek's traditional hunting grounds. By 1805, the Indians in this region of the South had ceded more than 2 million acres to the U.S. government. They had also begun to look to the English for support in their resistance to American settlers.

On his journey to the Creek in 1811, Tecumseh pressed for a southern confederation similar to the one he was shaping among the northern tribes. He did not win as many converts to his idea as he had hoped, particularly among the older chiefs. But his message won followers among a younger faction, known to Americans as the Red Sticks for the red war clubs they carried. Unlike their elders, the Red Sticks were eager to take on their white enemies.

A series of incidents soon strengthened this war party. Tecumseh had supposedly warned the older chiefs that if they did not accept his message, "they would hear the stamp of his foot when he returned to Canada." Soon after he left, a series of earthquakes rocked the Tennessee-Georgia area. To many Creek, this seemed to confirm Tecumseh's supernatural powers. Then the following year, 1812, a Red Stick chief named Little Warrior led a band of Creek north to visit Tecumseh. The band arrived in time to take part in the Raisin River massacre. On their way back south, the Red Sticks murdered two unsuspecting white families. Continuing their journey home, they bragged about their deed and showed off their scalps and booty.

When Little Warrior reported his exploits to the older Creek chiefs, they ordered him from the council. Shortly after, the United States government demanded that Little Warrior and his companions be turned over to American authorities. The older chiefs refused, deciding that they would hand out punishment themselves. The guilty Indians were hunted down and shot or tomahawked. Many of the Red Sticks retaliated against this action by attacking whites in the area. A split was developing among the Creek that resembled the beginnings of a civil war.

Many of those who took up the Red Stick were of mixed European and Indian ancestry. William Weatherford, for example, was seven-eighths white, wealthy, and highly respected. He liked to boast that he was part Scotch, part French, and part Creek but had "not one drop of Yankee blood." Among the Indians Weatherford was known as Red Eagle.

In July 1813, Peter McQueen, another Red Stick of mixed European and Indian ancestry, visited Pensacola, Florida, with a band of 350 warriors to deliver a letter from the British to the Spanish authorities there. (Great Britain and Spain were allies in the fight against Napoleon.) According to McQueen, the Spanish governor agreed to give him "a small bag of powder each for ten towns, and five bullets for each man." This was "not more than enough for a hunting expedition," explained the governor. American settlers, however, thought otherwise and decided to take action. As McQueen's column halted at Burnt Corn Creek, 80 miles north of Pensacola, it was attacked by an American militia of 180 men. The surprise caught the Red Sticks off guard, and the Americans momentarily succeeded in seizing the pack horses. But as the Americans stopped to divide the booty, other Indians, scattered in the woods across the stream, opened fire. They scared off the Americans, recovered their pack horses, wounded 15 militiamen, and collected two scalps.

The Battle of Burnt Corn Creek turned out to be the opening battle of the Creek War. It changed what might have been a civil war among the Creek into a larger war against the United States.

McQueen promptly returned to Pensacola to obtain more ammunition and supplies from the Spanish. In the meantime, American settlers along the nation's southern frontier began taking refuge inside hastily constructed stockades. One such stockade was Fort Mims, on the Alabama River a little north of the Florida border. It sheltered 553 persons, including about 150 militia under Maj. Daniel Beasley.

On the night of August 29–30, a band of 1,000 Creek warriors led by Red Eagle quietly surrounded the fort. As commander, Beasley tended to be casual in his security. When Red Eagle learned that the stockade door was usually held open by drifting sand and that no sentries were posted, he devised a plan of action. Waiting until the inhabitants of the fort were eating lunch on August 30, Red Eagle's party sprinted through the open gate, whooping and hollering. Beasley's skull was smashed as he tried to close the stockade gate. The Americans, including the women, fought bravely for three hours until Red Eagle ordered his warriors to tip their arrows with fire and burn the houses and the people inside them. As the sun sank, 400 whites lay dead and mutilated on the ground. Most African Americans were spared to be used as slaves. One black woman managed

THE WAR IN THE SOUTH

Davy Crockett was among the Tennessee frontiersmen who joined General Jackson in the Creek War after the massacre of settlers at Fort Mims. *(Library of Congress, Prints & Photographs Division [LC-USZ62-93521])*

to escape and paddle a canoe down the Alabama River to Fort Stoddard with news of the disaster.

The August 30 massacre at Fort Mims galvanized Americans in Georgia and the Mississippi Territory. But the main force in the American drive against the Creek came from Tennessee. Within the month, some 2,500 Tennessee militia had gathered to invade the Creek homeland. Among them were Sam Houston, later to become governor of Tennessee and president of the Republic of Texas, and frontiersman Davy Crockett, "the merriest of the merry . . . [who kept] the camp alive with his quaint conceits and marvelous narratives." At the head of the expedition was Andrew Jackson.

Jackson was popularly known as "Old Hickory." He supposedly got the nickname when a soldier in his outfit commented admiringly, "He's tough as hickory." To which another soldier chimed in, "He's tough as *old* hickory." Jackson was determined to wipe out the hostile Red Sticks and then seize Florida. In an impassioned appeal for volunteers, he wrote:

Brave Tennesseans! Your frontier is threatened with invasion by a savage foe! Already do they advance towards your frontier, with their scalping knives unsheathed, to butcher your wives, your children, and your helpless babes. Time is not to be lost. We must hasten to the frontier, or we will find it drenched in the blood of our fellow-citizens.

Both the Creek and the Americans faced logistical problems. The Indians had no more than 4,000 warriors all told, and the most that ever entered a single battle was about 1,000. They had no artillery and only limited firearms. Since ammunition was hard to come by and they had little practice with the musket, they fought mostly with bows and arrows, tomahawks, and war clubs.

For their part, the Americans had to move supplies through 150 miles of roadless wilderness. To feed his 2,500 men and 1,300 horses, Jackson needed each week 1,000 bushels of grain, 20 tons of meat, 1,000 gallons of whiskey, and other miscellaneous provisions. Moreover, the term of service for the militia usually expired at the end of one year. Jackson had to threaten his troops to keep them intact. On two separate occasions, he leveled his gun against soldiers who wanted to go home. And on a third occasion, more than half of his army actually disbanded.

The first six months of the Creek War turned out to be inconclusive. In November 1813 the Creek were defeated at Tallassahatchie and again at Talladega, losing about 800 warriors. In both instances, Jackson used the tactic of forming his men into a semicircle, letting the Indians attack, and then closing the gap to encircle the enemy. But although the Americans had superiority in men and arms, they were confronting terrible conditions—inhospitable terrain, pestiferous insects, shortages of food. Jackson himself came down with dysentery. At one point, the governor of Tennessee wrote to Jackson suggesting that he retreat because of the difficulty of supplying his troops. Old Hickory was indignant.

Are you my Dear friend recommending to me to retrograde to please the whims of the populace? . . . Let me tell you it imperiously lies upon both you and me to do our duty regardless of the consequences of the opinions of these fireside patriots.

Over the winter of 1813–14, Jackson built his army up to 5,000 men, including 600 regulars and some friendly Choctaw and Cherokee Indi-

THE WAR IN THE SOUTH

Red Eagle, leader of the Creek Indians, surrenders to Andrew Jackson, ending the bloody Creek War. *(Library of Congress)*

ans. In February 1814, he learned that 1,000 Red Stick warriors, with 300 women and children, had fortified themselves on a peninsula called Horseshoe Bend on the Tallapoosa River. The land approach to the Horseshoe was protected by a zigzag rampart of logs five to eight feet high, with portholes through which the Creek could send out a withering crossfire. The river protected the Horseshoe on the other three sides. The Indians had set their canoes out along the river in case they had to flee. Jackson decided to attack.

On the morning of March 27, Jackson made his move. Silently, the friendly Choctaw and Cherokee swam the river and made off with the Creek's canoes. At 10:00 A.M., Jackson began pounding the enemy with cannon fire. At noon he launched a frontal assault. In the meantime, other American troops used the stolen canoes to attack the fort from the rear and set it on fire.

The Red Sticks, using war clubs and tomahawks, were slaughtered by the muskets, bayonets, and overwhelming numbers of the Americans. The battle lasted until nightfall. When it was over, 550 Creek warriors were dead, not counting those who had tried to escape by the river.

American losses were 32 killed and 99 wounded; the Indian "friendlies" suffered 18 killed and 36 wounded.

Shortly after, Red Eagle—once more known as William Weatherford—surrendered to Jackson at his headquarters. With the words "My people are no more!" Weatherford offered himself as a hostage. He sought mercy, however, for the starving Creek women and children. Always admiring a brave man, Jackson let him go and provided food and supplies for his people. Weatherford spent the rest of his life as a respected Alabama planter.

Jackson was far less generous to the full-blooded Creek. On August 9, 1814, he forced the tribal chiefs to sign the Treaty of Fort Jackson. The treaty took more than 20 million acres of land from the Creek, about one-fifth of Georgia and three-fifths of Alabama. Most of the Indians participating in the parlay had been friendly to Jackson and some had even fought on the American side. When they protested the treaty's terms, Jackson told them they had a choice: either to sign or to move to Florida, where most of the remaining hostile Creek had fled. The Treaty of Fort Jackson stripped both friend and foe, without discrimination.

Ever since his victory at Horseshoe Bend in March 1814, Jackson had been serving as head of the U.S. Army's Seventh Military District, which included Tennessee, Louisiana, the Mississippi Territory, and West Florida. And although the Treaty of Fort Jackson put an end to the conflict with the Creek, Jackson realized that he and his forces could contribute to the larger war with Britain. He had received reports that the British were gathering troops and ships at Pensacola in Spanish Florida. He had reason to believe that the British were going to use this force to attack New Orleans and that to do so they would first want to take Mobile, then a port in Louisiana. So late in August 1814, Jackson sent troops with heavy cannons to strengthen Fort Bowyer, which guarded the approach to Mobile. When the British did indeed try to enter Mobile Bay on September 15, they were driven off and sent back to Pensacola.

That was all Jackson needed as an excuse to attack Pensacola. He sought authorization from Washington to march into the Spanish-held colony. But permission never came. Instead, Secretary of State James Monroe wrote Jackson a letter, dated October 21, 1814, forbidding Jackson to attack Pensacola. President Madison, Monroe explained, did not want the United States to have to deal with another enemy in addition to Great Britain.

Jackson apparently received the letter only *after* the War of 1812 was over. But many historians think that he would have ignored it even if he had received it in time. To Jackson, Pensacola was essential to the defense of Mobile and New Orleans. It was the best harbor on the Gulf coast and

New Orleans

NEW ORLEANS WAS FOUNDED BY A FRENCH EXPLORER in 1718. Four years later, it became the capital of the French colony of Louisiana. Strategically located near the mouth of the Mississippi River, the settlement grew quickly. By 1763, when it was ceded to Spain, it was one of North America's leading ports.

Over the next several decades, the city boomed as white settlers poured across the Appalachians, fur traders moved throughout the Mississippi valley, and merchants bought and sold cotton, lumber, and other products. In 1800 Spain returned New Orleans to France. Three years later, the city became part of the United States as a result of the Louisiana Purchase.

When the War of 1812 broke out, New Orleans was perhaps the nation's most cosmopolitan city. About two-thirds of its population of 30,000 did not speak English. The predominant language was French. In addition to French, Spanish, and white Americans, its inhabitants included former black slaves, Indians, and immigrants from various Caribbean islands. Many people were creoles, of mixed European and black ancestry.

New Orleans was a lively place. Markets, shops, and theaters stayed open on Sundays. There were numerous gambling houses and coffeehouses. Among the popular amusements were animal fights, such as those billed as "Six Bull-dogs against a Canadian Bear" and "Twelve dogs set against a strong and furious Opelousas Bull."

Despite its attractions, New Orleans had one major disadvantage: disease. The city's swampy location made malaria an ongoing problem. The subtropical climate, plus the arrival of ships carrying infected water from West Indian ports, encouraged annual outbreaks of yellow fever. Sanitation facilities were extremely poor. Privies and wells for drinking water were usually situated close together, which meant that such diseases as cholera and typhoid spread rapidly. All in all, New Orleans was probably America's most dangerous city from the point of view of health.

was easily accessible to the interior of Florida. "Pensacola," Jackson said, "is more important to the British arms than any other point on our South or Southwest."

So without waiting for official word from Washington, Jackson called out the Tennessee and Mississippi militia and recruited some friendly Choctaw. By November 3, a total of 4,000 troops were ready for the march on Pensacola. Much-needed arms did not arrive on time because they were shipped by flatboat instead of steamer in order to save the contractor extra freight charges. Nonetheless, Jackson decided to go ahead.

On November 6, Jackson set up camp two miles outside Pensacola. He then demanded the surrender of the two nearby forts, which were staffed by British Royal Marines under Maj. Edward Nicolls. While the Spanish governor of Pensacola dallied over his response, Jackson made plans for an assault.

Seven British ships guarded the western approach to the city. So Jackson sent a small force to the western side to put the British off guard and brought the main body of his troops around from the east. After some brief but heavy fighting, the Spanish governor was forced to surrender. In disgust, the British blew up their forts and sailed away to Jamaica. Major Nicolls, however, fled toward the Apalachicola River, about 150 miles east of Pensacola. There he established a new base and continued to harass Georgia and West Florida for the remainder of the war. He also incited the Indians to raid settlements in U.S. territory.

Jackson, meanwhile, took his forces west to Mobile. By mid-November he had solid information from spies that the British were readying a large force in Jamaica to attack New Orleans. There was no mystery as to why the British would want to capture that city. Its location near the mouth of the Mississippi made it the commercial outlet for cotton, sugar, hemp, lead, tobacco, and other products from most of the country west of the Appalachian Mountains. Losing the city would be a disaster for the American economy as well as a blow to national pride.

So, leaving several regiments to guard Mobile in case the British tried to return there, Jackson set off overland on November 22 for New Orleans. The forces he was assembling were a mixed lot. The bulk of them were the "Kaintucks" and other rough backwoodsmen who wore deerskin or homespun suits and hats of fox and raccoon fur, with the animals' tails dangling to the rear. Their hair hung to their shoulders, they were covered with fleas, and their body odor was so strong that townspeople tried to keep upwind of them. They also drank a lot—whiskey rather than wine. On the other hand, they were armed with Kentucky long rifles instead of the standard musket. Muskets were short-range weapons, good up to 200 yards and not very accurate. Kentucky long rifles had spiral grooves cut into their barrels that gave their bullets a spin in flight. As a result, the long rifles were effective up to 300 yards and were far more accurate than muskets.

In addition to the Kaintucks, Jackson's army contained a mixture of people. There was a group of Choctaw Indians. There were French soldiers who had served under Napoleon and wanted nothing better than a second chance to fight the British. There was a corps of free blacks, including some from Santo Domingo. Jackson was indifferent as to where his soldiers came from or what they looked like. The important thing was how well they would fight. When an army paymaster held back the wages of nonwhite soldiers, Jackson told him in no uncertain terms that he was to pay wages promptly "without inquiring whether the troops are white, black, or tea."

Jackson's army even included a group of pirates from Barataria Bay in southern Louisiana. Since 1810, the pirates had been raiding Spanish ships in the Caribbean and smuggling the goods into New Orleans. In 1814 the British offered Jean Lafitte, the pirate leader, $30,000 if he would help them fight the United States. Instead, Lafitte sent a warning to the authorities at New Orleans and offered to help Jackson if the United States would later acquit the pirates on charges of violating American trade laws. The pirates turned out to be a great asset, for they brought cannons, powder, and ammunition with them and proved to be expert artillerymen. They also added 1,000 men to Jackson's growing army. Because they knew the local terrain so well, they became Jackson's source of information about topography and British ship and troop movements.

When Jackson arrived in New Orleans on December 2, 1814, he found the city ill prepared against attack. However, he also discovered that its location made it easily defensible. New Orleans was situated on a spit of dry land on the left bank of the Mississippi River, about 100 miles north of the river's mouth. Most of the surrounding countryside consisted of swamps filled with huge cypress trees, marshy reeds, and alligators and other wildlife. Here and there were winding waterways called bayous. Six miles east of the city was a shallow bay, Lake Borgne, which opened into the Gulf of Mexico.

Pirates

JEAN LAFITTE (CA. 1780–CA. 1825) WAS ONE OF THE more colorful characters of the War of 1812. It is believed he was born in France, but historians know nothing about his early life. By 1810, however, he and his brother, Pierre, were leading a band of pirates who raided Spanish ships in the Caribbean and then sold their plunder on the black market in New Orleans. Since Lafitte did not attack U.S. ships, the American authorities usually left him and his men alone. Once, however, the governor of Louisiana offered a $500 reward for Lafitte's capture. Mockingly, Lafitte offered a $30,000 reward for the governor's capture. Lafitte and his men fought bravely at the Battle of New Orleans. Six years later, in 1821, they sailed away and were never heard from again.

Piracy was an easy way to get rich during the 1700s and early 1800s. Merchant ships carried huge amounts of gold and goods across the Atlantic. Yet they were only lightly armed, in contrast to the heavily armed pirate ships. In addition, naval pay was low and living conditions aboard merchant ships were usually miserable. As a result, few sailors were willing to fight to protect a ship's cargo.

Pirate vessels likewise suffered from rats and poor rations. But pirates at least had the opportunity of making a great deal of money, since each crew member received a share of the captured loot. Furthermore, if a pirate lost a limb, he was usually considered a crew member for life and continued to receive part of his shipmates' spoils.

Another difference between pirate ships and those of the regular navy was the way they were governed. Pirate ships were run on a more-or-less democratic basis, with each pirate having a vote as to the ship's operations. Naval ships were run by a rigid chain of command, and ordinary seamen were expected to follow orders without question.

Jackson proceeded to seal off the various approaches to New Orleans. He placed heavy guns at the forts that guarded the city along the river. He used available men and slaves from nearby plantations to fell trees and fill the bayous with mud. And he set up a gunboat patrol on Lake Borgne. He also scouted positions where he could place troops quickly when a British attack came.

The cypress swamps surrounding New Orleans, such as this one at La Place, were difficult to navigate and served as natural obstacles to an attack. *(National Archives Still Pictures Branch, NWDNS-412-DA-3694)*

Meanwhile, the British had assembled an army of 14,000 men, including the soldiers who had burned Washington, D.C. With the death of General Ross at Baltimore, command of the army had been given to Maj. Gen. the Honorable Sir Edward Pakenham, a veteran of the Napoleonic Wars.

On November 30, a British fleet of 60 ships, commanded by Admiral Alexander Cochrane, sailed from Jamaica, where the army had been assembled, toward the Gulf Coast. In addition to five ships of the line and other warships, the fleet included barges to carry off loot from New Orleans' warehouses. The fleet also bore civilians who would be needed to administer the new British colony: tax collectors, secretaries, printers, and the like. Many of the army officers brought along their wives, complete with silk ball gowns for a victory celebration.

The fleet arrived at Cat Island, about 80 miles from New Orleans, in mid-December. Cochrane decided that the best way to attack the city was through Lake Borgne. He soon realized that the mouth of the lake was so shallow that he would have to use barges rather than warships to move the troops. In his way was a small flotilla of five American gunboats under the command of Lt. Thomas ap Catesby Jones. The American officer had been ordered only to keep an eye out for the British and report their coming to Jackson. But on December 14, the wind failed and the gunboats were becalmed. When the British approached, Jones had no alternative but to fight. The battle was fierce but brief. By noon, all five American gunboats had been taken. American casualties numbered six dead and 35 wounded, including Lieutenant Jones. British casualties were far higher, with more than 300 men killed and wounded.

With Jones out of the way, the British set up a base at Pea Island and began exploring the area in search of a route out of Lake Borgne to New Orleans. With the help of some Spaniards, they found it: a bayou called Bayou Bienvenue (meaning "welcome"). For some reason, Jackson's axe-men had failed to cut down trees to block it. Bienvenue led to a wide plain along the Mississippi River, eight miles below New Orleans.

On December 22, an advance force of 1,800 British soldiers set out in open boats to row the 30 miles from Pea Island to Bayou Bienvenue. All day long, a cold rain fell. In the evening, the temperature dropped below freezing, and the soldiers' wet uniforms turned stiff. By early morning of December 23, the boats finally reached shore. The British were now about 15 miles from their goal.

Around noon on December 23, the first British troops came out of the swamp and onto solid ground. There they saw a sugar plantation owned by the Villeré family. On the porch of the plantation house sat a young man, his feet on the railing, smoking a cigar. It was Gabriel Villeré, son of the plantation owner and a major in the Louisiana militia. Suddenly, Villeré noticed the flashes of red among the trees. Realizing that the enemy was approaching, he vaulted over the porch railing and dashed for the swamp, enemy bullets whistling over his head. He crossed the Mississippi, obtained a horse, and galloped as fast as he could to New Orleans.

By 2:00 P.M., Villeré had reported the arrival of the invasion forces to Jackson. The general's response was immediate. "By God, gentleman," he shouted, "we'll fight them tonight!" Church bells rang, drums called every able-bodied man to assembly, and within an hour Jackson was marching down the river road to the Villeré plantation with an army of 2,000 men. Moving along the river next to him was the schooner *Carolina*, carrying 14 guns.

By about 7:00 P.M., after dark, the Americans had taken up attack positions in the trees surrounding the British encampment. The *Carolina* anchored nearby. The British soldiers were gathered around

THE WAR IN THE SOUTH

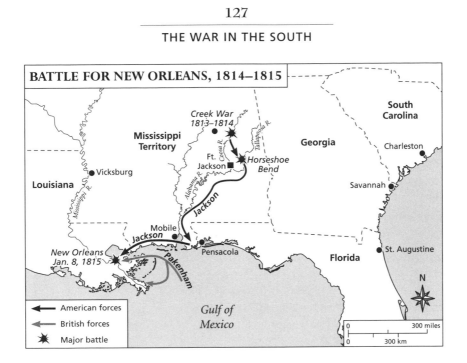

campfires, enjoying the warmth and rest. Even their commander, Maj. Gen. John Keane, a black-whiskered Irishman, was relaxed. After all, the Americans would never attack at night. It would be an uncivilized act, in violation of all the rules of European warfare and traditional military tactics. Keane obviously did not know Jackson.

At 7:30 P.M. the *Carolina* opened up a barrage of fire, catching the British completely by surprise. A British officer described the scene: "Flash, flash, flash, came from the river, the roar of cannon followed, and the light of her own broadside displayed to us an enemy's vessel at anchor near the opposite bank, and pouring a perfect shower of grape and roundshot into the camp."

At 8:00 P.M. Jackson moved forward to attack. Darkness, fog, and the thickening powder smoke made it almost impossible to tell friend from foe. The Americans fired wildly in the general direction of the enemy. The British, better trained and more experienced, stood stubbornly against the rush of the riflemen. Soon the two sides were mixing it up in hand-to-hand combat, with sword, knife, tomahawk, bayonet, and gun butt. For two hours the hit-and-miss fighting raged. Then Jackson ordered a general withdrawal, and by 10:00 P.M. the Villeré plantation was silent.

The Battle of New Orleans (*National Archives, Still Pictures Branch, NWDNS-111-SC-104311.*)

Losses were heavy on both sides. Some 217 Americans were killed and wounded. British casualties numbered 46 dead and 231 wounded. However, the battle was a psychological, if not a military, victory for the Americans. The British no longer felt so superior to the "dirty shirts," their nickname for the ragtag American militiamen.

From the Villeré plantation, Jackson pulled back about three miles to the Rodriguez Canal. This was a dry drainage ditch that ran for three-fifths of a mile from the cypress swamp to the Mississippi River, across the river road to New Orleans. Jackson put his men to work building a three-foot-high wall of earth and mud about 30 feet behind the ditch. On top of the wall, the Americans placed wooden platforms bearing cannons that were protected by thick bales of cotton.

On Christmas Day, American soldiers manning the wall could hear cheers from the British camp, heralding the arrival of General Pakenham with reinforcements from Jamaica. The Americans, too, were expecting additional troops. By the time all the reinforcements arrived on both sides, the British would have 9,000 men against Jackson's 5,000.

Pakenham realized that he could not move his troops closer to the Rodriguez Canal as long as the *Carolina* and the newly arrived *Louisiana* were offshore to fire at his line. So he ordered cannons brought up from Pea Island, and on the morning of December 27, the British artillery began raining shells on the two American ships. Suddenly a red-hot ball landed in the center of the *Carolina*'s hold. Fire from the shot spread rapidly and hit the magazine, which exploded with a roar loud enough to be heard in New Orleans. The *Louisiana* managed to escape.

On December 28, Pakenham launched a major assault against the American line, leading off with a bombardment of Congreve rockets. Jackson, seated on a white horse, rode along the line, shouting to his men that the rockets were "mere toys to amuse children." The line held fast. Then the British infantry attacked in row after row of tightly packed men. Within minutes, they were caught in a crossfire between the American guns along the canal and the guns of the *Louisiana*. Finally, realizing that his assault was getting nowhere, Pakenham ordered his troops to retreat. The morning's fighting cost him 150 men killed and wounded. American losses were nine killed and eight wounded.

Determined to try again, Pakenham ordered heavy naval guns brought up from Pea Island and placed behind an earthern emplacement. By December 31, 30 British cannons, supported by huge barrels filled with unrefined sugar rather than sand, were aimed at the American line.

British General Edward Pakenham died valiantly trying to rally his men in their retreat at the Battle of New Orleans. *(Library of Congress)*

On New Year's Day of 1815, in order to lift the spirits of his men, Jackson agreed to a full-dress parade to which the inhabitants of New Orleans were invited. But the mist cleared, and the British seized the opportunity to shower Jackson's headquarters on the Macarte plantation with hundreds of cannonballs. After the first surprise, American gunners began shooting back. The bombardment continued for more than four hours. The cotton bales the Americans had used to support their guns caught fire quickly and obscured the gunners' aim with clouds of black smoke. The barrels of sugar the British had used were shattered, and the sugar mixed with the rain that had begun to fall and made a sticky, slippery mess of the British position. By midafternoon, the "Battle of the Bales and Barrels" was over, more or less a draw. Wherever the British tried to outflank their enemy, the Americans were able to hold the line.

The fourth and final phase of the Battle of New Orleans took place on January 8, 1815. As the morning mist lifted, two British rockets exploded in the air to signal the attack. The British soldiers, dressed in their brilliant red coats and white belts, marched forward, a mass of color as far as the eye could see. It was a most impractical way to fight, but that was

African-American Soldiers at New Orleans

ALTHOUGH MANY BLACKS FOUGHT ON THE AMERICAN side during the Revolutionary War, after 1792 most states ruled that only whites could serve in their militia. However, Louisiana, although a slave territory, had a high proportion of free black inhabitants and, as a result, maintained a free black militia. Ironically, it was used mostly to hunt runaway slaves. Soon after 1803, however, it was disbanded.

In 1812 Louisiana became a state. With a British invasion looming, Governor William Claiborne wrote President Madison, recommending that the free black militia be recommissioned. Madison agreed, and Louisiana began recruiting a "Battalion of Free Men of Color." Although the law called for all militia officers to be white, the battalion had three black second lieutenants: Isidore Honoré, Vincent Populus, and Joseph Savary. Both Populus and Savary were later promoted to the rank of major.

In September 1814, Andrew Jackson issued a call to New Orleans's "freemen of color" to "rally round the standard of the eagle." He acknowledged past discrimination against blacks in the military and promised that it would no longer exist. He also promised black volunteers "the same bounty in money and lands now received by the white soldiers of the United States, viz: one hundred and twenty-four dollars in money, and one hundred and sixty acres of land."

Free blacks eventually made up two battalions of 200 to 250 men each. They were equipped by a wealthy New Orleans merchant, Col. Michel Fortier, Sr. The black battalions fought bravely during the Battle of New Orleans, suffering more than twice the number of casualties that white battalions did. One British officer wrote, "The New Orleans colored regiment were so anxious for glory that they could not be prevented from advancing over our breastworks and exposing themselves."

The aftermath of the battle, however, was disillusioning for black soldiers. They were forbidden to join in the victory parade, although Joseph Savary defied the order and marched his troops through New Orleans. Only a few black veterans received a pension, and there is no evidence that any of them received their promised bounty and land.

Andrew Jackson, hero of New Orleans and the seventh president of the
United States *(National Archives, Still Pictures Branch, NWDNS-208-PR-10P-2)*

how European soldiers had fought for centuries. Only in the Americas
had Europeans adopted a different style of warfare, one that took advantage of the wooded terrain.

Jackson waited until the enemy was within 500 yards. Then the American army band struck up "Yankee Doodle" and Jackson ordered his men to commence firing. A load of musket balls and scrap metal flew from the American cannons into the British lines, toppling 200 British soldiers at one stroke. Then the Yankee riflemen began to shoot. Jackson had stationed his men in four rows, one behind the other. As soon as the front row fired, they stepped back to allow the second row to fire, and so on. The result was a continuous, deadly barrage. At last, unable to keep their line, the redcoats began to flee. Pakenham bravely stuck his hat on a sword and ran forward, trying to rally his men. But he was cut in two by a cannonball. (His body was later shipped home in a cask of rum.) General Keane was shot through the throat. Finally, one of Pakenham's officers ordered a retreat, as the American army band played "Hail Columbia."

The slaughter was immense. The British suffered 700 dead, 1,400 wounded, and 500 captured. American losses stood at 13 dead and 39 wounded. Two days later, Jackson wrote to Secretary of War Monroe that "Last night at 12 o'clock the enemy precipitately decamped and returned to their boats."

As it turned out, the Battle of New Orleans had been completely unnecessary. For on December 24, 1814, the British and the Americans had signed a peace treaty in Ghent, Belgium, ending the War of 1812.

9

GHENT, HARTFORD, AND PEACE

It was perhaps fitting that the last battle of the War of 1812 was one that need never have been fought. If ever there was a war that need never have been started, it was this one. In both instances, the misstep was due to the unavoidable delay in those days of getting news across the Atlantic Ocean. But there were other broader and bitter ironies that pervaded this conflict.

Almost from the day the war formally began in June 1812, the two nations' leaders—realizing that the immediate causes could well be negotiated—started sending out peace feelers. As the conflict progressed, both sides either took the initiative to negotiate a peace or played a waiting game, depending on the outcome of each major military or naval action.

Then in March 1813, the emperor of Russia, Czar Alexander I, offered to mediate a settlement. Russia and Great Britain were at that time allies in the war against Napoleon, and the United States was one of Russia's main trading partners. President Madison sent Secretary of the Treasury Albert Gallatin, together with Senator James A. Bayard, a moderate Federalist from Delaware, to St. Petersburg, Russia, where they were joined by John Quincy Adams, the American ambassador to Russia. For six months the trio cooled their heels, waiting for word from the czar, before they learned that the British had refused the mediation proposal.

However, Britain's foreign minister, Lord Castlereagh, offered to negotiate directly with the American envoys. By January 1814, President Madison had agreed to this suggestion and Ghent, Belgium, was chosen as a neutral city where negotiations could take place. Madison sent Henry

John Quincy Adams headed the American delegation that met with French and British officials in Ghent, Belgium, to negotiate peace. *(Library of Congress)*

Clay, the young representative from Kentucky, and Jonathan Russell, the mature ambassador (then in Stockholm, Sweden) from Massachusetts, to join the other Americans.

The American team was a disparate and uncongenial group. Its head was John Quincy Adams, son of the nation's second president, a brilliant but humorless individual and a stickler for promptness. Senator Bayard described him as "singularly cold and repulsive. His manners are harsh and you seldom perceive the least effort to please anyone." Adams disapproved strongly of his colleagues' behavior. "I dined again at the table d'hôte," he wrote in his diary. "The other gentlemen dined together at four. They sit after dinner and drink bad wine and smoke cigars, which neither suits my habits nor my health, and absorbs time which I cannot spare."

Clay was charming, a lover of good wine and cigars, with a fine sense of humor. He was also a gambler, who often looked upon the negotiations with a gambler's eye and instincts. Adams recalled Clay's attitude when, at a later stage in the bargaining, the British retreated from some of their demands. Adams noted: "[Clay] asked me if I knew how to play brag [a card game]. I had forgotten how. He said the art of it was to beat your adversary by holding your hand with a solemn and confident phiz [face] and outbragging him." This was a ploy that Clay used on several occasions, probably to Adams's dismay.

Gallatin turned out to be the peacemaker. As his young son, who accompanied his father to Europe, described it: "Clay uses strong language to Adams and Adams returns the compliment. Father looks calmly on with a twinkle in his eye. Today there was a severe storm and Father said, 'Gentlemen, gentlemen, we must remain united or we fail.'" Bayard and Russell, while taking a back seat at the negotiations, got on well with their colleagues.

From the start of the sessions in August 1814, it was obvious that neither side wanted to bring up the controversial issue of impressment of sailors. Instead, both sides presented a list of demands. The British attitude was expressed in an editorial in the London *Times:* "Our demands may be couched in a single word—Submission!" The London *Courier* wanted the United States to give up its fishing rights in British waters and return Louisiana to Spain. Canada demanded that the United States also cede northern New York, part of Maine, and control of the Great Lakes. In addition, Canada pressed for the establishment of an Indian buffer nation along the Greenville Treaty line of 1795, to separate the United States from Canada. The Americans, on the other hand, wanted the United States to take over Upper Canada on the ground that "Experience has shown that Great Britain cannot participate in the dominion and navigation of the Lakes without incurring the danger of an early renewal of the war."

The negotiations dragged on for months. The British eventually abandoned the Indians and gave up their demand for creation of an Indian nation. They also agreed to return American territory they had captured. In turn, the Americans withdrew their demand for Canadian territory. Since they were holding out on the impressment issue, only two points of dispute remained. One was American fishing rights in Canadian waters. Because Adams came from New England, whose local economy depended greatly on fishing, he was loath to make any concession on the matter. The second point of dispute was a British claim that they had the right to navigate the Mississippi River. Since the river was the key to western commerce, it was now Clay's turn to be infuriated by the British demand. Adams, on the other hand, was willing to go along. "The navigation principle," retorted Clay, "is much too important to concede for the mere liberty of drying fish on a desert." Finally, it was agreed to postpone discussion of the questions of the fisheries and the Mississippi. Eventually these and other issues would be settled peacefully by special commissions and treaties.

As the negotiations dragged on in Ghent, events and attitudes in North America proceeded on their own course. And despite the victories of the Americans on Lake Champlain and the withdrawal of the British forces from the Chesapeake Bay region—both events occurring in September 1814—many Americans were becoming increasingly impatient with the war. Nowhere was this impatience more tangible than in New England.

Many New Englanders had been opposed to the war from the beginning. Yet although they complained about the war, New Englanders had generally carried on commercial traffic with the enemy. Boston bankers lent money to the British. Vermont farmers drove their cattle across the border until it was estimated that two-thirds of the British army in Canada were eating beef furnished by American contractors. The Salem, Massachusetts, *Gazette* noted that smuggling had become "the most lucrative business which is now carried on." In September 1814, the British governor of Nova Scotia, Gen. Sir John Sherbrooke, took possession of much of Maine (which was then part of Massachusetts) from Passamaquoddy to the Penobscot River. Instead of resisting, most inhabitants of the Maine coast shrugged their shoulders, swore an oath of allegiance to King George III, and went about their business.

At the same time, economic conditions in the United States were worsening. The prewar embargo had previously ruined thousands of Americans. Now the British blockade of the country's eastern seaboard was strangling American commerce, while the costs of running the war were skyrocketing. In fact, the government had so little revenue that soldiers went unpaid, the interest on the national debt fell into arrears, and there were almost no funds to support the diplomatic corps overseas or to provide for the care of American prisoners of war in England.

The American army was not only suffering from a lack of funds. It did not have enough manpower to wage the next campaign, and desertion was a serious problem. Secretary of War Monroe believed the answer lay in creating a larger army composed of regulars. Congress agreed and suggested two things: a draft and giving 18-year-olds permission to volunteer without the consent of their parents. Both proposals caused a furor in New England. Why should the New England states send taxes to Washington to pay for a national army and, at the same time, pay to

Busy dockside scenes like this one in 1790s Salem, Massachusetts, were conspicuously absent in the United States from 1808 through early 1815 due to both the 1807 U.S. embargo and the British blockade of U.S. ports. *(Library of Congress)*

support their state militia? On the contrary, the United States government should pay for the services of the state militia. Monroe finally agreed, but only if the state militia were placed under the command of regular army officers. Whereupon the governors of Massachusetts, Connecticut, Rhode Island, and Vermont indignantly refused on the grounds that Monroe would order the troops out of New England and into Canada. As for permitting 18-year-olds to enlist without parental consent, that was "another wicked scheme on the part of the Southerners and Westerners . . . to destroy the very foundation of the American home by encouraging boys to defy the authority of their parents."

The situation was complicated by party politics. The Federalists—who had lost the last four presidential elections to the Republicans—looked forward to the day when their party would once more take power in Washington. A leading Federalist in Congress, Representative Daniel Webster of New Hampshire, was willing to concede that the War of 1812 was necessary *if* it was waged on the ocean for "free trade and seamen's rights," but he could not accept a war in which the idea of annexing Canada was dominant and American commerce was being destroyed. Most New England Federalists agreed with him. However, attempts to put a Federalist in Madison's cabinet had failed, and it seemed unlikely that the Federalists had enough power to influence national policy.

So to air their concerns and seek possible solutions, New England Federalists adopted a procedure that had been used prior to the birth of the United States. They called for a convention. The call went out to the New England states on October 6, 1814, to meet in Hartford, Connecticut, on December 15 in order to obtain "security against Conscription, taxes & the danger of invasion" and to restrain "the tendency to excess."

Connecticut, Massachusetts, and Rhode Island sent delegates. Federalist leaders in New Hampshire and Vermont opposed the idea of a convention, but two New Hampshire counties sent delegates and one delegate from Vermont was seated, bringing the total to 26. The proceedings, which were held in secret, lasted for three weeks and aroused considerable comment in the national press. The Boston *Sentinel* spoke for the Federalists when it declared that "The tyrannical oppression of those who at present usurp the power of the Constitution is beyond endurance." New England was advocating two principles of states' rights: interposition, under which a state might oppose any federal action it believed encroached on its sovereignty, and nullification, which meant that a state would not enforce a federal law with which it disagreed. In contrast, southern newspapers like the Richmond, Virginia, *Inquirer* denounced nullification as treason. Ironically, 45 years later, North and South were to reverse their positions on this issue as the nation headed toward civil war.

The Hartford Convention discussed secession but decided to drop the matter. Instead, the convention ended with the suggestion of seven amendments to the U.S. Constitution. In general, the amendments were designed to meet New England's regional problems and resentments. For example, one amendment stated that no government agency could enforce an embargo for more than 60 days. Another amendment called for apportioning congressional representatives and direct taxes according to the number of free persons in each state, thus strengthening the political power of northern free states and lessening that of southern slave states. Still another amendment stated that a president could not come from the same state as his predecessor, a clear blow against the so-called Virginia dynasty of Thomas Jefferson and James Madison.

How far all these matters were from the original causes of the war! Here were New Englanders apparently more at odds with their own government and constitution than with the British and their policies. Indeed, the more extreme Federalists had actually gone to Hartford prepared to

The Treaty of Ghent, which ended the War of 1812, was signed December 24, 1814, but news of it did not reach the United States until February 11. *(National Archives, Still Pictures Branch, NWDNS-111-SC-96965)*

threaten secession and a separate peace if they did not get their way. In the end, though, the moderates such as Harrison Gray Otis of Massachusetts had prevailed. A restrained statement was drawn up on January 5, 1815, and three members of the convention were chosen to present its "requests" in Washington.

But once more, the delay in communications was crucial. No one in Hartford or anywhere else in North America could know that the delegates in Ghent had signed a treaty ending the war on December 24, 1814. It was a Christmas present that many British and American soldiers and sailors would never live to enjoy. The news did not reach New York by ship until February 11, 1815. On February 12, the very day that the three "ambassadors" from the Hartford Convention were riding through Philadelphia on their way to the nation's capital, messengers from Andrew Jackson were entering Washington with news of the stunning American victory at New Orleans. Only on February 13 did riders enter Washington with a copy of the treaty from Ghent. When the ambassadors from Hartford arrived in the midst of the ensuing celebrations, they quickly muted their demands, but the irreparable damage to the Federalist Party had been done.

On February 16, the Senate ratified the treaty by a unanimous vote of 35 to 0, and President Madison signed it the same day. The War of 1812 was officially declared over on February 17, 1815, at 11 P.M. It is not recorded when word of this event reached England, but in any case there, too, the war had come to be regarded as just as futile and unpopular as it seemed to so many Americans.

Which side won the war? Because they had defeated the British at New Orleans and on Lake Champlain and had driven enemy forces from the Chesapeake region, the Americans declared themselves victorious. The Canadians, having lost none of the territory the Americans set out to capture, considered themselves winners. Once and for all, too, the outcome of the war would disabuse those who believed that Canada might join the United States. Since the peace treaty did not deal with either impressment or the rights of neutral shipping in wartime—Madison's original reasons for declaring war—even the British could claim some sort of victory.

A series of negotiations in the years following the war resulted in treaties between the United States and Britain that produced some of the very results that might have been expected without resorting to combat. The Rush-Bagot agreement of 1817, for instance, set limits on the naval forces that the United States and Canada could maintain on the Great Lakes. A long series of negotiations, commissions, and treaties would eventually settle the disputed boundaries between the United States and Canada from Maine to Oregon. The issue of American fishermen's rights off Canada's maritime provinces proved more difficult and still leads to disagreements. But although there have been many minor confrontations involving fishermen and Coast Guard forces, neither side has ever seen the need to resort to war.

Casualties during the War of 1812 were just light enough to be acceptable on both sides. About 1,900 American soldiers and sailors were killed in action (although that many must also have died from wounds, given the state of medicine in those days). British casualties, both those killed and wounded, were about the same—almost half of them sustained at New Orleans. About another 1,000 American civilians probably lost their lives—mostly in attacks by Indians supporting the British.

But the real losers of this war were the Indians—and not just the hundreds who had lost their lives in battle. The war consolidated the gains made from the "treaties" that Americans had imposed on the Indians before and during the war itself—establishing once and for all that Native Americans could not look to the British to help them hold, let alone regain, their tribal lands in North America. Equally important, the fact that some Indians had fought with the British only strengthened some Americans' belief that the Indians could not be trusted to live alongside expanding white settlements. Andrew Jackson, for one, would not rest until he defeated the Seminole Indians in Florida. He later presided over the removal of thousands of Indians in the southeast to western lands.

Another group whose fate was immediately affected by the war of 1812 were the African Americans who were still slaves in the United States. In a little-cited term of the Treaty of Ghent, both the United States and Britain agreed to "use their best endeavors" to abolish the slave trade in Africans. As a matter of fact, slave traffic had been formally abolished by the U.S. Congress in 1808. However, neither this law nor the Treaty of Ghent's term actually stopped the importation of African slaves into the American South. But above all, the War of 1812, by suddenly opening up more territory in the South and West to white settlers, led to the formation of more slave states. The Missouri Compromise which followed in 1820 was an attempt to accommodate these new slave states, but it only postponed the inevitable reckoning, the Civil War. If the War of 1812 had anything relevant to say to Americans, it was that it is easier to tackle a major foreign military power than domestic social problems.

There is no denying, however, that the United States emerged from the conflict with a strong feeling of national pride. For the second time in some 30 years the former colonies had resisted the actions of their former master. As Albert Gallatin put it: "The war renewed and reinstated the National Feelings and character which the Revolution had given, and which were daily lessened. . . . [The people] are more American; they feel and act more as a nation."

The increase in national pride bolstered the sense many Americans had that they were destined to rule the continent "from sea to shining sea." The end of the war inspired more and more Americans to keep pushing westward. For example, the census of 1810 had shown 24,520 residents in what was then the Indiana Territory. By 1815 there were 63,897 residents. And the following year, Indiana became a state. Three new states joined the Union in the next three years: Mississippi in 1817, Illinois in 1818, and Alabama in 1819. The westward movement was to continue throughout the 19th century.

Within a few years of the war's end, the United States also expanded southward. Many Americans had always assumed that Spanish Florida would eventually join the Union, and as soon as the War of 1812 ended,

Indian Removal

MOST WHITE AMERICANS CONSIDERED INDIANS "savages" who stood in the way of their own hunger for land. The result was a series of wars that by about 1800 resulted in whites obtaining most Indian land east of the Mississippi River.

In 1803 Thomas Jefferson introduced the idea of resettling the eastern tribes on land west of the Mississippi. In 1804, when the Louisiana Territory was organized, the act contained a provision to this effect. Both James Monroe and John Quincy Adams continued Jefferson's policy of encouraging resettlement.

Andrew Jackson, however, felt that Indian removal was proceeding too slowly. So in 1830 he persuaded Congress to pass the Indian Removal Act, under which all Indians living east of the Mississippi were to be forced to migrate west of the river, mainly to the territory that would eventually become the state of Oklahoma. The land there was considered worthless for farming, which meant that white Americans would not be interested in it.

Three groups of Native Americans refused to sell their land and move. They were the Sauk and Fox, the Seminole, and the Cherokee. Both the Sauk and Fox and the Seminole fought the United States. But they were defeated and most of them ended up in either Iowa or Oklahoma. The Cherokee did not fight. Instead, they appealed to the U.S. Supreme Court on the grounds that a 1791 treaty guaranteed their independence and therefore the Georgia government could not remove them from their ancestral lands. The court ruled in their favor. Andrew Jackson, however, refused to allow federal troops to protect the Indians. "[Chief Justice] John Marshall has made his decision," the president reportedly said. "Now let him enforce it." In 1838 the Cherokee were forced to move to Oklahoma. About 4,000, or one out of four, died from cold, hunger, or disease on the forced march along what is now known as the Trail of Tears.

they started moving in. In 1817 armed conflict broke out between the settlers and Seminole Indians and black slaves who had fled to freedom from Georgia. President James Monroe put Andrew Jackson in charge of an army to bring peace to the area. Jackson's idea of peace was to burn every Indian village he could find, capture Pensacola from the Spanish

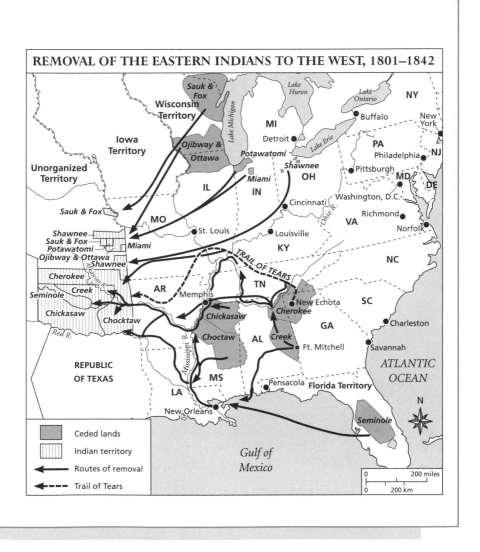

REMOVAL OF THE EASTERN INDIANS TO THE WEST, 1801–1842

for the second time, and hang two British subjects whom he suspected of having helped the Seminoles. After much negotiation, the dispute was settled peacefully. Under the Adams-Onís Treaty of 1819, the United States acquired Florida from Spain in exchange for $5 million. However, the Seminoles continued to resist the United States until 1842.

After the war ended, Andrew Jackson commanded U.S. troops in Florida, waging brutal war on the Seminole Indians. *(Library of Congress)*

Another result of the War of 1812 was a realization that the United States had to be prepared to fight. As President Madison said, "Experience has taught us that a certain degree of preparation for war is not only indispensable to avert disasters in the outset, but affords also the best security for the continuance of peace." Accordingly, Congress passed a law setting up a permanent peacetime army of 10,000 men. A general staff to lead the army was created. Appropriations were made to build additional forts along the frontier. And Congress authorized the spending of $8 million for construction of nine ships of the line and 12 frigates. Within three months of the signing of the peace treaty at Ghent, the U.S. Navy, led by Stephen Decatur, sailed to the western Mediterranean and put an end to the activities of the Barbary pirates

A war requires weapons, and the Royal Navy's blockade meant that Americans had been unable to obtain muskets, cannons, and gunpowder from their usual sources overseas. As a result, a domestic armaments industry developed. The industry received its biggest boost when Eli Whitney devised a system of using interchangeable parts in the manufacture of guns. For example, the barrel of a gun could be made that would fit all other guns. Whitney received a government contract for 10,000 muskets and secured enough other contracts to open a factory at Whitneyville, near

New Haven, Connecticut. From there, the "American System" of manu-facture spread to other industries and other parts of the world.

The war also marked the end of Jefferson's dream of an agrarian soci-ety. By 1815 even he admitted that a viable economy required a balance between agriculture, manufactures, and commerce. In 1816 Congress passed the nation's first protective tariff. Soon new industries were springing up in all parts of the country. For example, Pittsburgh's iron began to replace British and Swedish iron, while imported jute was driven out by bagging woven in Kentucky out of local hemp.

Protectionism was combined with internal improvements. In 1815 President Madison delivered a message to Congress in which he under-scored "the great importance of establishing throughout our country the roads and canals which can best be executed under the national author-ity." The development of these federal roads and waterways encouraged a transportation revolution that in the years after the war provided set-tlers going west and south with faster and safer means of travel.

Part of the transportation revolution included the growth of steam-boat traffic on the western rivers, especially on the Mississippi. In 1816, 40 shiploads of merchandise, valued at $8 million, passed through New Orleans. Within five years, steamboat commerce would double the city's trade. Rice, cotton, tobacco, grain, and other products from the United States found their way to a hungry European market and helped propel the United States to a position of economic strength.

Waterways built during the War of 1812 became thoroughfares for steamboats carrying goods to foreign markets. *(Library of Congress)*

The war also forged the future leadership of the nation. One battle alone, the Battle of the Thames, was fought with the participation of one future vice president, three governors, four senators, and 20 congressmen. Andrew Jackson, William Henry Harrison, and Zachary Taylor all served in the military during the War of 1812 and later became president of the United States. Other prominent figures of the war would also become president—James Monroe, Madison's secretary of state, and John Quincy Adams—but their prominence had less to do with their conduct in the war than with their efforts in making peace. Three other men whose reputations were made in Congress during the war ran for president—Henry Clay, John Calhoun, and Daniel Webster—and although they were never elected president, their influence on the national scene during the years leading to the Civil War was enormous.

General Winfield Scott would also ride the crest of his courageous actions in the war, and although he failed in his bid for the presidency, he remained a genuine American hero for five decades. The war also produced three naval heroes—Oliver Hazard Perry, David Porter, and Stephen Decatur—four, actually, including Capt. James Lawrence, killed when the *Chesapeake* was defeated by the *Shannon*. The war also confirmed another hero. When the USS *Constitution* was about to be destroyed in 1830, a 21-year-old medical school student, Oliver Wendell Holmes, composed a stirring poem entitled "Old Ironsides": "Oh, better that her shattered hulk/Should sink beneath the waves," he declaimed, than that this once-proud ship should be dismantled. His poem aroused public sentiment. The vessel was rebuilt and restored to service, and it survives to this day as one of America's inspirational icons.

Perhaps what the United States gained from the war was best summed up in a Vermont newspaper in 1815:

> The fear of our late enemy;
> The respect of the world; and
> The confidence we have acquired in ourselves.

Glossary

barrel   The tubelike part of a gun through which the bullet travels.

battalion   An army unit, usually consisting of two or more companies.

bounty   The payment given by a government to someone who enlists for military service.

bow   The front section of a ship or boat.

breach   To break through an enemy's lines or defensive works.

breastwork   A defensive wall.

brig   A two-masted, square-rigged sailing ship.

broadside   The firing at the same time of all the guns on one side of a ship.

broadside song   Words printed on a single sheet of paper and sold for a penny. The purchaser then fitted the words to a popular tune.

bulwarks   The part of a ship's side that is above the upper deck.

cannon   A large, fixed mounted gun.

cartridge   A small lead ball used as ammunition in a musket.

cat-o'-nine-tails   A length of tarred, knotted rope used to whip sailors in the British navy.

chain shot   Two balls joined by a chain formerly used as a cannon charge; as they flew through the air, the chain ripped anything it came across.

Congreve rocket   A tube of sheet iron filled with gunpowder set off by a fuse. It made a tremendous noise when it was fired. It was named after its English inventor, Sir William Congreve (1772–1828).

crow's-nest   A small lookout platform with a railing, located near the top of a ship's mast.

cutlass   A short heavy sword with a curved, single-edged blade that was used by sailors.

decimated   Originally referring to the killing of every tenth individual, it has come to refer to the killing of a large proportion of a group.

deploy   To position troops in readiness for combat.

dry goods   Textiles.

emplacement   A fixed and prepared gun position.

evangelical Protestantism   A form of Protestantism that emphasizes personal conversion and enthusiastic preaching based on the four gospel books of the New Testament.

flank   In military jargon, the side of an army's force. The left or right flank of the enemy describes the side from the viewpoint of the attacker.

flintlock   A gun that is fired by a small hammer striking on flint, which produces a spark to ignite the powder.

flotilla   A naval unit smaller than a fleet but larger than a single squadron. It may also refer to a fleet of small ships.

foundering   Filling with water and sinking.

frigate   A high-speed, medium-sized sailing warship, carrying from 28 to 44 guns on one gundeck.

gangrene   The decay and death of body tissue due to infection. When it occurred in an arm or a leg, the limb usually had to be amputated.

grapeshot   Small iron balls formerly used as a cannon charge; on exploding, the small shot scattered far and wide.

grappling ropes   Ropes with iron hooks on one end that were used for grasping and holding, especially for holding an enemy ship alongside.

hull   The body of a ship, excluding any parts above the main deck.

inaugural address   A speech delivered by a president or other high government official when he or she is inducted into office.

indemnity   A payment for damage or loss.

kedging   A technique for moving a sailing vessel by means of a light anchor; the anchor is thrown as far away as possible in the desired direction, and when it grips the bottom, the ship pulls itself forward.

logistics   In military science, the organizing and transporting of supplies and equipment needed for battle.

GLOSSARY

magazine A storeroom where ammunition is kept.

mandate An authorization or instruction.

mast A tall vertical pole that rises from the deck of a sailing vessel to support the sails and the rigging.

maverick One who is politically independent.

musket A muzzle-loaded firearm with a smooth bore, good for short-range shooting. In the early 1800s it was still being fired with a flintlock action.

planking A number of wooden boards fastened together to serve as the deck of a ship.

privateer A privately owned and manned vessel that has been commissioned by a government to attack and capture enemy ships.

ramrod A long, thin steel pole used to insert a cartridge down the barrel of a musket.

recommission To put a ship back into active service.

reconnoiter To explore in order to gain military information.

redcoat A nickname for a British soldier deriving from the color of his uniform's coat.

rifle A shoulder gun with a barrel whose interior has been spirally grooved (rifled); rifling greatly improves the accuracy and range of bullets.

rigging The system of ropes, chains, and tackle used to support and control the masts and sails of a sailing vessel.

salvo The firing of several guns at the same time.

schooner A sailing vessel with at least two masts, the front mast being smaller than the rear mast.

scurvy A disease caused by the lack of vitamin C. Its symptoms include weakness and bleeding gums. For many centuries it was an ailment of sailors who spent lengthy periods at sea without fresh foods.

scuttle To sink a ship on purpose.

sector A military area.

septicemia A disorder caused by bacteria invading the bloodstream. Its symptoms include high fever, chills, low blood pressure, and confusion. It often spreads to other organs, such as the lungs, liver, and brain, and can be fatal.

seventy-four   A large sailing warship carrying between 64 and 120 cannons mounted on three gundecks.

short-staple cotton   Cotton with fine, short fibers.

shot   Ammunition for a cannon or firearm.

sloop   A single-masted sailboat.

sniper   Someone who shoots from a concealed vantage point.

solid shot   Large iron balls formerly used as a cannon charge.

spar   Any of several wooden poles used to support sails and rigging on a sailing vessel.

stalemate   A situation in which neither side can accomplish anything.

stern   The rear part of a ship or boat.

strategist   A military planner.

subordinate   A person lower in rank than another.

tar   A sailor. Possibly derived from *tarpaulin,* possibly from the dark, oily material used to seal and protect the wood of ships from water.

tick   A mattress cover.

Further Reading

NONFICTION

Baker, Kevin. "The Shores of Tripoli." *American Heritage.* February/March 2002, pp. 17–18.

Banfield, Susan. *James Madison.* New York: Franklin Watts, 1986.

Bosco, Peter O. *The War of 1812.* Brookfield, Conn.: Millbrook Press, 1991.

Buckley, Gail. *American Patriots.* New York: Random House, 2001.

Caffrey, Kate. *The Twilight's Last Gleaming.* New York: Stein and Day, 1977.

Carr, Caleb. "Americans Don't Understand That Their Heritage Is Itself a Threat." *The New York Times Magazine.* September 23, 2001, pp. 91–92.

Clinton, Susan. *James Madison.* Chicago: Children's Press, 1986.

Cwiklik, Robert. *Tecumseh: Shawnee Rebel.* New York: Chelsea House, 1995.

Dunn, John. *The Relocation of the North American Indian.* San Diego, Calif.: Lucent Books, 1995.

Edmunds, R. David. *The Shawnee Prophet.* Lincoln: University of Nebraska Press, 1985.

Falkner, Leonard. *For Jefferson and Liberty.* New York: Alfred A. Knopf, 1972.

Gilbert, B. "The Battle of Lake Erie." *Smithsonian.* January 1995, pp. 24–28.

Gordon, John Steele. "Driving a Soft Bargain." *American Heritage.* September 1996, pp. 16–18.

Greenblatt, Miriam. *John Quincy Adams.* Ada, Okla.: Garrett Educational Corporation, 1990.

Gruppe, Henry E., and the editors of Time-Life Books. *The Frigates.* Alexandria, Va.: Time-Life Books, 1979.

Hickey, Donald R. *The War of 1812: A Forgotten Conflict.* Chicago: University of Illinois Press, 1989.

Immell, Myra H., and William H. Immell. *Tecumseh.* San Diego, Calif.: Lucent Books, 1997.

Kent, Zachary. *Tecumseh.* Chicago: Children's Press, 1992.

Larkin, Jack. *The Reshaping of Everyday Life.* New York: Harper & Row, 1988.

Leavell, J. Perry, Jr. *James Madison.* New York: Chelsea House, 1988.

Leckie, Robert. *The War Nobody Won: 1812.* New York: G.P. Putnam's Sons, 1974.

Malone, Mary. *James Madison*. Springfield, N.J.: Enslow Publishers, 1997.

Marden, L. "Restoring Old Ironsides." *National Geographic,* June 1997, pp. 8–53.

Marrin, Albert. *1812: The War Nobody Won*. New York: Atheneum, 1985.

Martin, Tyrone G. *A Most Fortunate Ship: A Narrative History of "Old Ironsides."* Chester, Conn.: Globe Pequot Press, 1980.

Morris, Richard B. *The War of 1812*. Minneapolis, Minn.: Lerner Publications, 1985

Nardo, Don. *The War of 1812*. San Diego, Calif.: Lucent Books, 2000.

Park, E. "Our Flag Was Still There." *Smithsonian.* July 2000, pp. 22–26.

Perret, Geoffrey. *A Country Made by War*. New York: Random House, 1989.

Pickles, Tim. *New Orleans, 1815: Andrew Jackson Crushes the British*. London: Osprey, 1993.

Phelan, John. *The Burning of Washington*. New York: Thomas Y. Crowell Company, 1975.

Remini, Robert V. *Andrew Jackson and the Course of American Empire: 1767–1821*. New York: Harper & Row, 1977.

———. *Andrew Jackson and His Indian Wars*. New York: Viking, 2001.

Santella, Andrew. *The War of 1812*. Danbury, Conn.: Children's Press, 2001.

Sheads, Scott. *The Rockets' Red Glare: The Maritime Defense of Baltimore in 1814*. Centerville, Md.: Tidewater Publishers, 1986.

Shorto, Russell T. *Tecumseh and the Dream of an American Indian Nation*. Englewood Cliffs, N.J.: Silver Burdett, 1989.

Stefoff, Rebecca. *William Henry Harrison*. Ada, Okla.: Garrett Educational Corporation, 1990.

———. *Tecumseh and the Shawnee Confederation*. New York: Facts On File, 1998.

Sugden, John. *Tecumseh's Last Stand*. Norman: University of Oklahoma Press, 1985.

Tallant, Robert. *The Pirate Lafitte and the Battle of New Orleans*. New York: Random House, 1951.

Thom, James A. *Panther in the Sky*. New York: Ballantine Books, 1990.

Todd, Anne. *The War of 1812*. Mankato, Minn.: Capstone Press, 2001.

Wallace, Anthony E. C. *The Long, Bitter Trail: Andrew Jackson and the Indians*. New York: Hill and Wang, 1993.

Whitehorne, Joseph A. *The Battle for Baltimore 1814*. Baltimore, Md.: Nautical and Aviation Publ, 1996.

FICTION

Benton, Amanda. *Silent Stranger*. New York: Morrow/Avon, 1998.

Cabral, Olga. *So Proudly She Sailed*. Boston: Houghton Mifflin, 1981.

Forester, C. S. *The Captain from Connecticut*. Baltimore, Md.: Nautical and Aviation Publ., 1997.

FURTHER READING

Jennings, John. *The Salem Frigate.* New York: Doubleday, 1946.

Rinaldi, Ann. *Broken Days.* New York: Scholastic Books, 1997.

Williams, Ben Ames. *The Scarlet Thread.* Boston: Houghton Mifflin, 1939.

WEBSITES

"Star-Spangled Banner and the War of 1812." Available online. URL: http://www.si.edu/resource/faq/nmah/starflag.htm. Downloaded on March 27, 2002.

"The War of 1812 and Tecumseh," Bkejwanong Walpole Island First Nations Website. Available online. URL: http://www-personal.umich.edu/~ksands/War.html. Downloaded on March 27, 2002.

"The War of 1812," U.S. Army Website. Available online. URL: http://www.army.mil/cmh-pg/books/amh/amh-06.htm. Downloaded on March 27, 2002.

Index

Page numbers in *italics* indicate a photograph. Page numbers followed by *m* indicate maps. Page numbers followed by *g* indicate glossary entries. Page numbers in **boldface** indicate box features.

INDEX

INDEX

INDEX

WAR OF 1812

INDEX